For Brownies Everywhere

SBN 361 03511 X
Copyright © 1976 by PURNELL BOOKS
Berkshire House, Queen Street, Maidenhead,
Berkshire. Made and printed in Great Britain by
Purnell & Sons Ltd., Paulton (Avon) and London

Cover picture shows Lindsay Sanderson of the 1st. Prestwood, Bucks, Pack.
Endpaper photographs by Dr. B. Forman and the *Oxford Mail*.

The Brownie Annual 1977

Published by special arrangement with
THE GIRL GUIDES ASSOCIATION

PURNELL

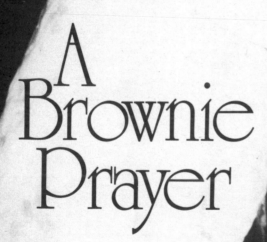

A Brownie Prayer

by Jean Howard

Thank you, God,
   For the gift of sight,
For the sun and the rainbow
   And the clear morning light.

Help me, God,
   To be cheerful and gay
And do at least one
   Good turn every day.

Teach me, God,
   To be patient and true,
To think first of others,
   Less of *me*, more of *You*.

Thank you, God,
   For the wind and the sea,
For firelight and moonlight,
   And caring for ME.

The 1st Hightown Brownies set out for their Pack holiday one very wet day in August. No one minded the rain except, perhaps, the Brownie Guider, Mrs Luce, who was worried that the bedding might get wet. Although the Brownies had been told to make sure it was in a waterproof covering, one or two bundles had rather flimsy covers. However, the luggage was all safely stowed in the boot of the coach. The Brownies climbed inside, and as the coach moved off a group of mackintosh-clad mums, small brothers and sisters waved goodbye.

The Brownies did not know then that Mary was watching from her window. Mary was particularly interested because she badly wanted to be a Brownie. She was a lonely and very shy girl, and she'd

The Brownies did not know then that Mary was watching from her window

Pack Holiday Adventure

by Doris Bellringer

never found the courage to ask to join the Pack. Her mother, who went out to work, never guessed how much Mary longed to be a Brownie, even though Mary had mentioned she wished she was one.

It happened that Mary was going to stay for a holiday with her grandparents, who lived quite near to Pack Holiday House.

When the Pack arrived at their destination the rain had stopped, the sun was shining, and raindrops were glistening on the hedges. Underfoot it was still very wet, so Mrs Luce asked the Brownies to make a line from the door of the coach to the door of Pack Holiday House. This looked like a very

long snake as all the luggage was passed from one to the other so that nothing—well, hardly anything!—touched the wet ground.

Once inside, the Brownies sorted out their cases and took them to the bunks, which had already been labelled with their names. It was fun getting unpacked and making up the beds. Sue wanted to go to bed straight away, although it was only five o'clock, but she and the others settled for bouncing up and down, using the bunk as a trampoline. They had to be careful not to bounce too high, though.

Next day they discovered a stream. This was quite shallow, but it bubbled merrily over boulders, with willow and elder

trees on the bank. One willow-tree was overhanging, so Sue, who was always adventurous, climbed up and swung herself right across the stream. As she jumped to the bank the branch sprang back and there she stood, quite alone, on the far side of the Pack grinned at her across the water.

"Come on!" she called. "It's lovely here", but no one else would chance going across by the branch.

Gradually it dawned on Sue that she could not get back as easily as she had crossed. The other Brownies wandered along the home side while Sue kept pace with them, searching all the time for a crossing-place. The river

7

It was very cold paddling through the water

did the water come higher than her knees. The rest of the Pack, relieved to have Sue back, were curious about Mary. Sue told them that she was staying in a country cottage with her grandparents, but she did not admit that it was Mary who had shown her how to get back. In spite of her adventurous spirit, Sue had really been quite scared.

The Brownies soon had the feeling that Pack Holiday House was their real home, and the week just flew by. On the day before they were due to go home, Mrs Luce suggested a picnic by the stream. There was much bustle as the Elves and Sprites swept and dusted and the Kelpies prepared rolls and sandwiches. At last all was ready. Pack Holiday House was locked up, and they all set off for the picnic. They explored the stream again, and this time everyone paddled. They caught freshwater shrimps and tiny tiddlers, which they kept in a jamjar until it was time to pack up. Then the tiddlers were all tipped back into

Brownie Pack. There are the others, over there. Do you know how I can get back?"

Mary laughed, and Sue was glad she hadn't let her see how scared she was. "There's a little bridge, but it's quite a long way up— nearly to the next village," answered Mary. "But I usually paddle across."

Sue felt very silly, because she hadn't thought of this for herself. She was quite grateful, though, as she took off her shoes and socks and waved goodbye to Mary. Paddling through the stream, it was very cold, and the sharp stones hurt her feet, but nowhere

widened, the trees grew sparse, and then Sue realised that she was not alone. She was being followed by a girl in a pink dress.

"Hello!" shouted Sue. "What's your name?"

"Mary," answered the girl. "What's yours?"

"I'm Sue, and I'm here with our

the stream, for, with all the luggage, it would not be possible to take them back on the coach.

To finish the day everyone voted to play fifty-two bunker. The Elves all shut their eyes while the others went off to hide. There were marvellous places for concealment, and two Brownies reached "home" without being seen, which was something they never managed to do when they played at school. After the Sprites and Kelpies had had a turn there was a chorus of "You now, Brown Owl," and "Come on, Tawny", so Mrs Luce, Tawny and Cooky shut their eyes while all the Brownies ran off to hide themselves.

"Forty-nine, fifty, fifty-one, fifty-two, bunker!" chanted Mrs Luce, and with a great shout of "Coming!" she and the other two opened their eyes to find—no Brownies, of course! Suddenly in the silence which followed their shout they heard an agonised cry from the woods.

"Help, help!"

Without stopping, Mrs Luce,

Tawny and Cooky ran as fast as they could towards the woods and the voice; but someone else reached it first. This was Mary, who had waded swiftly across the stream to the rescue.

Sue had found a splendid place to hide in—a hollow tree—but inside the tree was a wasps' nest, and Sue disturbed the very lively inhabitants. She shrieked as angry wasps buzzed round her head. Quite terrified, she beat at them, and she might have suffered severely from stings if Mary hadn't rushed to the tree and pulled her out of the hollow.

The wasps followed, buzzing furiously about the heads of both girls.

"Run!" cried Mary, and still

holding Sue's arm she raced for the stream. "I know where it's deeper," Mary gasped out. "Wade in and duck under the water!"

Hand-in-hand, they ran into the stream, regardless of getting soaking wet. Mary guided Sue a few yards upstream and then plunged head-first in. The water formed a pool here between two

The wasps followed, buzzing furiously about the heads of both girls

9

"I'm sure we all wish you belonged to our Pack"

and three feet deep, and Sue, who could swim, had no hesitation in ducking her head under, where the wasps could not reach her.

One or two wasps were still buzzing about when the girls lifted their heads above the surface, but the danger was over, and they scrambled out to be greeted by Mrs Luce and the other two Guiders.

The Brownies soon joined the group.

"What a wonderful thing you did!" said Mrs Luce to Mary, when Sue told breathlessly what had happened. "If you hadn't thought of rushing into the stream Sue might be in quite a bad way now. We are all very grateful to you

for what you have done. You showed great courage and alertness. I'm sure we all wish you belonged to our Pack."

"Could I — oh, could I belong?" asked Mary, almost in a whisper.

"Well, not our Pack, I'm afraid," said Mrs Luce. "We are here on Pack holiday, so we should be much too far away for you to join when we leave."

"I live near you," said Mary shyly.

Then Sally, Sixer of the Kelpies, stepped forward. "Please, Brown Owl, I know Mary now. She's Mary Fenley, and she lives quite near us."

Then, slowly, it all came out — how Mary had longed to be a

Brownie but hadn't plucked up courage to ask to join.

"There's no lack of courage in you, of that I'm quite sure," said Mrs Luce. "Of course you can join our Pack, Mary, if your mother will let you. When we get home we'll go and ask her, shall we? In the meantime, while we are here you can spend the day with us. Would you like that?"

Mary was not backward in saying she would — very much — and when the Pack returned from the holiday Mrs Luce gained the consent of Mrs Fenley for Mary to become a Brownie. Each Six wanted her to be a Kelpie — or an Elf — or a Sprite! In the end she joined Sue's Six — the Sprites.

which Six reaches the Toadstool?

by Daphne M. Pilcher

One of the Sixes reaches the toadstool. Can you work out which one it is? You may cross the lines.

how to make a garden picture

by Ruth Hoult

You will need 1 white ceiling-tile or a piece of white cardboard about 23 cm (9″) square, paints, a long brown envelope, 2 sheets of white notepaper, glue, and an old magazine with lots of coloured pictures in it.

First divide the tile or cardboard into two halves by drawing a pencil-line faintly across the middle. Paint the top half blue for the sky and the bottom half green for the grass. Then leave to dry.

Draw the tree shape on the brown envelope and cut it out. The tree should reach from the bottom of the picture to within 2.5 cm (1″) of the top.

Draw the shapes of the cloud and the trees in the distance on the white notepaper. Make them nice and big and cut them out. Paint the trees in the distance dark-green and leave to dry.

Now for the flowers. Look through the magazine for brightly coloured pictures. Cut out all the coloured parts which have no words on them. Use these to cut out lots of flower shapes. Each flower should be as big as a 10p piece. Cut out four small triangles too. These are for the butterflies. Now cut out lots of leaves. Leaves can be any colour you like.

Finally the fence. Using the notepaper, cut out lots of thin white strips about 5 cm (2″) long. Then cut out a few strips the full length of the notepaper. These are the long pieces for the fence.

Now you are ready to stick everything into place. You can see the positions from the drawing. The tree is stuck into position first, then all the leaves, next the cloud and the trees in the

distance, then the flowers and the butterflies, and lastly the fence. Stick the short strips first, then the long strips right across the top of them. You may find you have to join some of the long strips together so that they will reach right across the picture.

Lastly, draw in the centres of the flowers, the bodies of the butterflies, and the lines for the bark of the tree and the lines on the trees in the distance. Your picture is now complete.

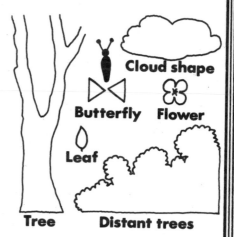

Tree   **Cloud shape**   **Butterfly**   **Flower**   **Leaf**   **Distant trees**

Garden Picture

A's for the *Apron* I'm going to put on,
B I'm a *Brownie* with jobs to be done.
C is for *Cooking* the cake that I make.
D is for *Dancing*, a badge I can take.

E's *Everybody*, the people I know,
F is for *Fun* when to Brownies I go.
G is for *Guiding*, to which I belong,
H *Hands* for helping, as I grow up strong.

I is for *Ideas* to serve God and Queen,
J is for *Journeys* — on badges we're keen.
K is for Knives, passing "Safety at Home",
L *Lend a Hand*, doing things on my own.

"*F is for Fun* when to Brownies I go"
Photo: Miss W. J. Beer

A Brownie Alphabet

With Music

by Patricia Durnall

M is for *Mother*, whom we try to serve,
N is for *Nature* we love to observe.
O is for *Olave*, the Lady B.-P.,
P's *Pack and Promise* for Brownies like me.

Q is for *Queen* and her family we know.
R is for *Revels*, to which Brownies go,
S is for *Service* that we try to do,
T is for *Trefoil*, our badge bright and new.

U is for *Union*, the flag of our land,
V is for *Ventures*, when all Lend a Hand.
W's *World*, Brownies two million there,
X *Green X Code*, roads safe everywhere.

Y is for *Yellow*, the tie that we wear,
Z is for *Zeal* in showing we care.
So in Brownie Guiding, in all that we do,
We try to be helpful and honest and true.

Hedgehog at the water's edge having a drink

Photograph by Michael Edwards

My Animal Friends

by the Editor

If you don't live on a farm or in the country, you may think that cows are dull animals and perhaps a little bit frightening when they stare at you as you walk through their field.

In fact, cows are quite interesting animals. They are nervous and timid, but they are so inquisitive that very often their curiosity overcomes their fear.

There is a herd of about four-teen cows in the meadow adjoining the house I live in, and sometimes the whole fourteen stand by the barbed-wire fence between the meadow and my garden and watch with close attention as I trim the hedge.

One day I offered the nearest cow a sprig of the hedge. She sampled it carefully and decided it wasn't bad. She must have thought I might be more tasty,

because she pushed her head between the barbed wire and licked my hand. I patted her, then stroked under her neck with a piece of hedge. She loved this; she closed her eyes blissfully, and lifted her head up for more.

I had to get on with my work, so I turned and went on trimming the hedge. As I moved along the hedge, I realised I'd caught my jacket on the barbed wire. I turned to release it, but found it wasn't on the barbed wire; my friend the cow had got the end of it in her mouth and was tugging at it.

One day a pig found its way into the cows' meadow. What astonishment it caused! I don't think the cows could ever have seen a pig before, because the whole herd was overcome with curiosity. They all followed the pig over the field. Where the pig went the cows went—mostly in single file, keeping a respectful distance behind the pig, who took not the slightest notice of them.

I think the pig finally found its way back through the fence, and peace again reigned in the meadow.

My cat, Winky, often brings fieldmice that he has caught into the garden, but one afternoon an unusual guest arrived. He didn't come in by the front door or even by the back. He came up, so to speak, from the basement. The first I knew of his arrival was seeing Winky pawing at something on the lawn. When I investigated, I saw that it wasn't something on the lawn, but something moving *under* the lawn. It was a mole. I couldn't see it, but I could follow it by the movements of the earth.

I love all our wild creatures, and although moles do damage to lawns I didn't want Winky to kill

Hare

Photo by N.H.P.A.

it, so I took the cat indoors. Then I flattened out the little hillock the mole had made and stamped it well down. Then I sat down in a deck-chair and had a snooze.

When I woke up, there was a fine molehill in front of my eyes. While I slept, Mr Mole had been busy tunnelling under the lawn. Not wanting the lawn disfigured, I fetched a spade and dug the "gentleman in the velvet coat" out. He squeaked loudly when I caught him, but I was only removing him for his own good, as I hope he realised when he found himself back in his own meadow.

I put food out regularly for the many birds that come into my garden, but one or two uninvited guests sometimes drop in for a snack. One morning I saw a tiny brown shape run out from the hedge, snatch up a piece of food and race back with it. It was a fieldmouse.

One evening, long before dusk, I looked out of the window and saw, feeding contentedly on the lawn, a baby hedgehog. To my dismay, Winky suddenly appeared. The hedgehog promptly rolled itself into a ball. Winky sniffed at it, but didn't try to penetrate the ball of prickles. When Winky had gone, the hedgehog unrolled itself, had a leisurely feed, and then ambled off into the hedge.

One day, to my astonishment, I saw a fine big hare sitting in the meadow opposite the house. I watched him for several days, then he disappeared.

Do remember that the wild creatures of our countryside need your care and protection. Look upon them as friends and neighbours who share the world with us. It is our privilege to help them live with their families safe from persecution, uncaged and free.

—R.M.

Photo: Robert Moss

I hose water into their trough for my friends the cows

Brownie Calendar

by Marcia M. Armitage

In January pantomimes are always quite the rage,
And Brownies simply love the chance to act upon the stage.
With lines to learn and clothes to make it's such a busy time,
But all agree that they enjoy our Brownie pantomime.

In February Thinking Day is what we celebrate;
We always look upon it as a very special date.
We think of Brownies far away and in our own land too;
We learn about the way they live and what they like to do.

In March you'll find that Brownies are all working very hard
To prepare a surprise present and design a pretty card,
Then on that certain Sunday you can hear each mother say
How nice it is to have a gift when it is Mother's Day.

In April with some hard-boiled eggs we have a lot of fun;
We decorate them first to see who makes the nicest one.
Then up a nearby slope we climb, and when Brown Owl says "Go!"
We roll the gaily painted eggs into the grass below.

In May we have a Nature Trail through woods of new spring green,
For at this time of year we find there's so much to be seen.
The birds are nesting secretly, but sometimes you may see
The baby birds with open mouths all chirping greedily.

In June midsummer Revels are the signal for some fun;
There's songs to sing and games to learn and races to be run.
We meet with other Brownies and so make some new friends;
But no one likes the moment when the Brownie Revels ends.

In July there's the Summer Fair to keep us very busy;
We're making items for the stall until we feel quite dizzy.
But, goodness, when we've sold it all we feel a glow of pride
And pleasure in a job well done by every Brownie Guide.

In August it's Pack Holiday, the highlight of the year;
The wind can blow, the rain can fall, the sun can disappear,
But we always enjoy ourselves in any kind of weather;
And Brownies on Pack Holiday love doing things together.

September brings in more recruits; we help them understand
About the Law and Promise, Brownie smile and Lend a Hand.
And now they're Leprechauns and Gnomes and Elves and Kelpies too
We think of new Pack Ventures and exciting things to do.

October and it's Hallowe'en, the night when witches ride
And black cats, ghosts and demons flit around the countryside.
In horrible disguise we dance by turnip-lantern light.
Why don't you come and see us? It's such a ghostly sight!

November 5th is Bonfire Night; we have a party where
Brown Owl has all the fireworks and sets them off with care.
It's much safer for an adult to set them off this way,
So no one is in danger and all enjoy the grand display.

December we sing carols at a home where old folk live.
Brown Owl takes a Christmas cake, and we've made gifts to give.
We go to church and look upon that scene of long ago,
To the sound of organ music playing carols soft and low.

A Brownie year is busy, but as well as all the fun
There's lots of useful things to learn and badges to be won.
We try to do our best for all — that's what a Brownie's for,
And all year round we try to keep our Promise and our Law.

"And Brownies simply love the chance to act upon the stage"
(1st Shenfield, Essex, Brownies present their "Cat Show")

Colour slide by Mrs. P. Bangert

"We go to church and look upon that scene of long ago"
Colour transparency by Alan T. Band Associates

Brownies in the Enchanted Wood

by Tilly Wingrave

"**O**nly one more day left!" sighed Sue, staring out of the window.

"But we've had a lovely time," said Mandy, perched on the edge of her bed, "even if it has rained every day."

"We haven't had a chance to explore the enchanted wood," grumbled Sue, looking across the wide lawn of the Brownie Pack Holiday House to the wood beyond.

"How do you know it's enchanted?" asked Mandy.

"I know!" replied her friend. "You only have to look at it to see that."

Privately, Mandy thought that Sue had rather too much imagination! Supposing she was right, though? It would be exciting to find out!

"Well," she said aloud, "you may get your chance tomorrow. The forecast is for fine weather, so Titania says we can go for a ramble in the woods with the Fairies."

"Titania" was the Brownie Guider. The "Fairies" were four Ranger helpers, who the Brownies called Peasblossom, Cobweb, Moth and Mustardseed, after the Fairy Queen's attendants.

The tinkling of handbells ("fairy music", the Brownies called it)

put an end to thoughts of exploring, and the girls ran down to supper.

The next day was warm and sunny.

"Put on your wellingtons," said Titania, as the Brownies prepared for their ramble. "It's sure to be wet in the woods."

"You mean our magic seven-league boots," corrected Sue.

"Of course!" smiled Titania. "How silly of me!"

The Brownies set off across the gardens and into the woods, with Peasblossom and Mustardseed leading the way, Cobweb nearly halfway along the line, and Moth

"You want to find out if the wood is enchanted, don't you?"

**...she saw to her amaze-
ment that the building
was a castle!**

bringing up the rear.

As they reached the woods, Sue caught Mandy's hand and began to drop back.

"What are you doing?" asked Mandy, as Sue stooped and pretended to look at something on the ground.

"Shh!" hissed Sue.

She watched as the Brownies disappeared round a bend in the path. Moth was listening to something a small Brownie was telling her, and hadn't noticed the two girls falling behind.

Pulling Mandy after her, Sue dived down a side turning.

"Come on!" she said. "You want to find out if the wood is enchanted, don't you?"

Mandy nodded. "Yes, but I don't think we ought—" she began, but Sue was already hurrying down the path.

Mandy ran after her. She found it hard to keep up with her longlegged friend. Then, rounding a bend, she saw that Sue was nowhere in sight.

Which way should she go? Quickly Mandy made up her mind, and hurried along the path to her right. After some time the trees began to thin out, and she caught a glimpse of a building in a clearing.

"Good!" she thought. "I'm back at the House."

But when she emerged from the trees she saw to her amazement that the building was a castle!

Was the wood magic, after all?

The doors of the Throne Room were flung open, and a very grand footman, carrying a magnificent silver punchbowl, came slowly down the room.

Mandy gave a gasp of horror as the footman caught his toe in the edge of the beautiful scarlet-and-gold carpet, and fell flat on his face. The punch spilled out in all directions!

"Bother!" grumbled Old King Cole. "Ah, well, send in my fiddlers three!"

There was a long pause, and then came the sound of raised voices in the distance. At last, after quite a time, the footman came back. He looked very red and flustered.

"Well," said the King, "where are they?"

"Er – I'm afraid——" began the footman.

"Where are they?" King Cole demanded. He was getting quite upset.

"I'm afraid they're on strike, Your Majesty," answered the footman nervously.

"Oh, bother, BOTHER!"

She crept forward and peeped in through a window. What she saw made her gasp in astonishment.

Old King Cole sat on his throne, wriggling to get comfortable.

"Bring me my pipe!" he called.

He settled his crown more firmly on his head.

As he did so, a worried footman appeared.

"I'm very sorry, Your Majesty," he said. "I'm afraid there has been an accident. The page who was bringing your pipe was tripped up by one of the royal cats, and your pipe was broken."

"Oh, well, I suppose it can't be helped," said Old King Cole, who was clearly disappointed. "Bring in my bowl."

. . . fell flat on his face. The punch spilled out in all directions

Now King Cole looked really cross. "This is really too bad!" He sat with his chin in his hand, not looking at all like the Merry Old Soul he was supposed to be.

Mandy felt very sorry for him. "I wish I could help," she thought.

Then an idea came to her. She began to creep round the castle, peeping through windows as she went. It wasn't long before she found the castle kitchen. Slipping in through an open door, she spoke quickly to the plump, rosy-cheeked woman inside.

Five minutes later she was back outside the Throne Room window.

"Now," she thought, "I hope the King is watching."

Old King Cole looked up. Something bright and shining was floating past the window. Looking out, he saw Mandy, with a clay pipe and a bowl of soapsuds, blowing bubbles.

"My word, that looks fun!" cried the King. He stepped out into the garden to have a closer look. "I suppose you haven't got a spare pipe?" he asked Mandy wistfully.

"Why, yes, Your Majesty, I have!" replied Mandy, and she held up a second clay pipe, which the royal cook had given to her with the bowl of soapsuds.

Old King Cole sat down on the grass beside Mandy. Soon each was happily trying to blow bigger and finer bubbles than the other.

"You know," said King Cole, after a time, "this really is fun. All I miss now is the music of my fiddlers three."

Without a word, Mandy reached into her pocket, and brought out the little transistor radio that Mummy and Daddy had given her for her birthday. The cheerful sound of music filled the castle garden. Soon the Queen and her ladies, and all the courtiers, came out to listen.

Hearing the music, the fiddlers three came into the garden. They were soon playing happily, their strike forgotten.

Old King Cole blew an extra

They sat together happily, each trying to blow better bubbles than the other

fine stream of bubbles. "You know," he said, watching the Queen and her ladies dancing, "this has turned out to be the merriest day I have ever spent!"

Picking up her radio, Mandy slipped away unnoticed into the wood.

When Sue realised that Mandy was no longer following, she at once turned back to look for her. In and out of the trees she hurried, but there was no sign of her friend. Not only that, before long she herself was completely lost!

At last she heard footsteps hurrying towards her. To her relief, round a bend in the path came Mandy.

"Oh, Sue," cried Mandy, as soon as she was near enough, "I've had such an adventure!"

Sue was both pleased and disappointed when she heard her friend's story.

"I knew the wood was enchanted!" she cried. "But I wish I had been with you," she added wistfully.

"It must be nearly lunch time," said Mandy. "Which is the way back?"

"I don't know," Sue confessed. "I'm lost. Let's try this way."

The two girls set off, but the path they were following seemed to twist and turn on itself, taking them deeper and deeper into the wood.

Suddenly Sue ran forward. "Look!" she cried. "We're back at your castle!"

"Wait!" called Mandy. "It's not the same one!"

As the Brownies stared at the castle's greystone walls—

"Oh, no—not again!" cried a voice, and a flock of blackbirds flew from an open window, and disappeared above the trees.

Moments later, a figure in velvet and ermine and wearing a gold crown ran from the door and stood watching the birds as they flew away.

"Can we help you, Your Majesty?" asked Sue politely.

"It really is too bad!" grumbled the King. "Just because I was pleased when the cook put four-and-twenty live blackbirds in the pie on my birthday she does it every week!" He straightened his crown. "After all," he went on, "when you're feeling hungry it's not very nice to see your dinner flying out of the window!"

"Come back to our Pack Holiday House and have lunch with us," said Sue impulsively. "I know Titania will be pleased to see you."

. . . a figure wearing a gold crown ran from the door and stood watching the birds

22

"Thank you—that's very kind of you!" replied the King. "Which way do we go?" He was obviously hungry!

"Oh, dear, I forgot!" gasped Sue. "We're lost!"

"You need never be lost in the enchanted wood," answered the King. "Just stand one on each side of me, and hold my hands. Now think hard of the place you want to go to." The Brownies gripped the King's hands. "Keep your eyes shut tight," he warned.

As the girls closed their eyes, they felt wind rushing past their faces; then there was a gentle bump.

"Now open your eyes," said the King.

To their surprise, the Brownies found themselves, still clutching the King's hands, walking along the path which led to the garden of the Pack Holiday House. Ahead they could see the rest of the Pack. Moth was still listening to the small Brownie.

Cobweb dropped back to speak to Moth. "Don't let the Brownies dawdle," she said. "We don't want to be late today. Lunch on the last day of a Pack holiday is always fun."

This was Moth's first Pack holiday. "Why," she asked, "what happens?"

"Miss Andrews, the District Commissioner, always comes," answered Cobweb. "She's great fun. She always dresses up as a fairy-tale character, and really enters into the spirit of things. Then, after lunch, she slips away before the Brownies find out who she really is." Cobweb looked round. "Where's that tall chatter-box and her little friend?" she asked anxiously.

"Here they come now," said Moth, as Sue and Mandy rounded the last bend. "But who's that with them?"

"It must be Miss Andrews," said Cobweb. "I suppose she came through the woods to meet us. She does look funny with whiskers."

Back at the house, the warm smell of lunch met them at the door. The Brownies quickly washed and hurried to the dining-room.

"Who was it the Brownies brought to lunch?"

Mandy and Sue were most surprised to find that their guest seemed to be expected. Titania, however, was a little puzzled when the King insisted on sitting between his two new friends!

Afterwards, the King drew them to one side.

"That was delicious," he said, "but I must hurry away now. I have a busy afternoon in the counting-house."

After the Pack had gone upstairs for the quiet hour, Moth gave a gasp.

"Oh, dear, I forgot!" she said to Titania. "A letter came for you by hand, just before we went out. I'll go and fetch it, shall I?"

She ran into the hall, and picked up an envelope from the brass tray on the table.

Titania opened it. "Why," she exclaimed, "it's from Miss Andrews! She says she won't be able to come to lunch today."

She looked up from the letter and stared at the Rangers.

"If she couldn't come," she said slowly, *"who was it the Brownies brought to lunch?"*

Brownie Badges of Other Lands

by
Mavis K. Huartson

Can you link up each Brownie badge with the country to which it belongs? Follow the strings carefully from the names to the badges

home and away

Chinese Brownies at Pack meeting in far-away Hong Kong

Photograph by Miss E. Paterson

Brownies of the 1st South Baddesley Pack, Hants., with guinea-pig and rabbit pets

Photograph by W. L. Westcott

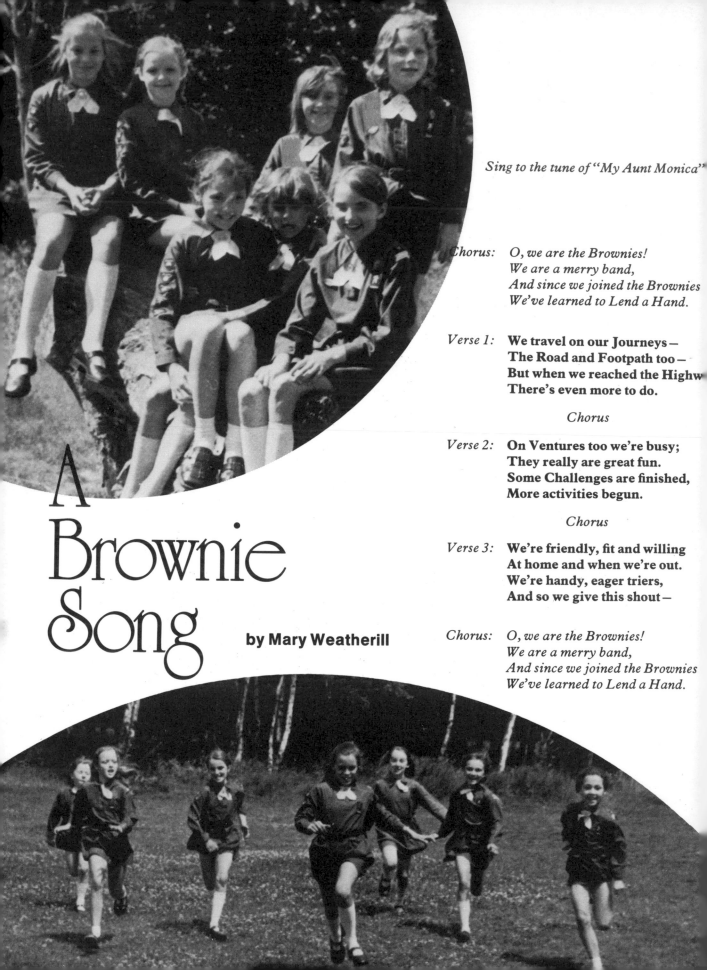

A Brownie Song

by Mary Weatherill

Sing to the tune of "My Aunt Monica"

Chorus: O, we are the Brownies!
We are a merry band,
And since we joined the Brownies
We've learned to Lend a Hand.

Verse 1: We travel on our Journeys —
The Road and Footpath too —
But when we reached the Highw
There's even more to do.

Chorus

Verse 2: On Ventures too we're busy;
They really are great fun.
Some Challenges are finished,
More activities begun.

Chorus

Verse 3: We're friendly, fit and willing
At home and when we're out.
We're handy, eager triers,
And so we give this shout —

Chorus: O, we are the Brownies!
We are a merry band,
And since we joined the Brownies
We've learned to Lend a Hand.

At Home and Abroad

Brownies with pet rabbits and dogs at the 1st Penrhyn Bay Pack's pet show, Carnarvonshire

Photos by Christine E. Foster

Brownie cowboys and Indians of the Gütersloh District Packs, complete with totems made by themselves, gather in readiness for the Westphalian Divisional Revels

Photo by Ann Hirschfield

the island of Flowers

by Susan Leng

Which of the five ships succeeds in reaching the Island of Flowers? This island is said to be full of rare and beautiful flowers, but no ship has ever managed to reach it, because whirlpools and dangerous currents keep all ships away unless they steer a secret, roundabout course to it. Which ship reaches it and where do the other four end up? Follow the compass directions and find out.

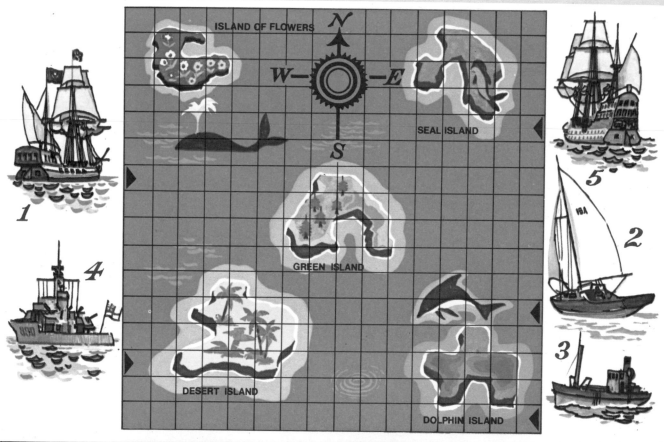

(1) PIRATE SHIP			(2) SAILING BOAT			(3) FISHING BOAT			(4) NAVAL SLOOP			(5) GALLEON		
3	squares	E	2	squares	W	6	squares	W	1	squares	E	3	squares	W
2	"	S	2	"	N	5	"	N	2	"	SE	6	"	S
1	"	E	2	"	SW	1	"	NE	7	"	E	2	"	SW
5	"	S	5	"	W	6	"	N	2	"	E	1	"	W
1	"	N	3	"	S	1	"	E	5	"	NW	3	"	SE
			6	"	W				7	"	N	3	"	N
			2	"	NE				2	"	W	1	"	
			1	"	E									

28

Brownie Anglers

Who was Miss Muffet?

P. Thompson Tells You

Little Miss Muffet of the nursery-rhyme was Patience, the daughter of a man who was interested in spiders and made a study of them. Patience lived in the sixteenth century. She had good reason to be frightened of spiders, for in those days they were sometimes used to "cure" illnesses and had to be swallowed live. Ugh!

Many nursery-rhymes have been passed on by word of mouth from one generation to another. It isn't easy to find out when they were first written down, but about two hundred years ago, in 1765, John Newbery published *Mother Goose's Melody*, also called *Sonnets for the Cradle*. These contained nursery-rhymes. A few years later another book of rhymes, called *Gammer Gurton's Garland*, was printed.

Some nursery-rhymes are useful in teaching children to count and to name familiar objects. "One, two, buckle my shoe" is an example. Some, like "The house that Jack built", are "adding-on" rhymes; these are found all round the world, not only in Great Britain.

Did you know that the nursery-rhyme "Ring a ring o' roses" began during the Great Plague of London? The "pocket full o' posies" were herbs carried to keep away infection, and "we all fall down" refers to the many people who died of the plague.

A real-life nursery-rhyme character was the King of Spain's daughter, who had "a little nut tree". She was Joanna of Castile and she visited the court of Henry VI in 1506.

Jack Horner is said to have been a dishonest steward. On his way to Henry VIII he opened a huge pie in which the Abbot of Glastonbury had put the title-deeds of several manors. He pulled out one for himself—the "plum" of the "pie".

If you lived in Sweden you would look for Jack and Jill in the moon. The Scandinavian legend tells how Hjuk and Bil were caught up to the moon while drawing water from a well, and can be seen there still, taking the place of our "man in the moon".

Mary's little lamb has always been a favourite in nursery-rhymes. Some young creatures adopt the first person or animal they see as their "mother" and follow closely everywhere whoever it is. Sheep act in this way, so if a young lamb is fed from a bottle by one of a farmer's family for a time it will often attach itself to that person even when it if fully grown. This sometimes turns out to be a great nuisance! Anyway, that's why "Everywhere that Mary went the lamb was sure to go."

So when you say or sing a nursery-rhyme to a young brother or sister, remember there's often an interesting story behind it.

The day King looked

December the twenty-sixth is the day on which, according to legend and the Christmas carol, good King Wenceslas looked out and saw a poor man gathering fuel. It is also St. Stephen's Day, the day on which Stephen was martyred by being stoned to death, but is best known to us as Boxing Day.

The name Boxing Day began to be used in the Middle Ages. It

Wenceslas ~~ut~~

by L. Baker

arose from a custom that came down from the Romans.

The Romans used to collect money from those who could afford it towards the cost of their athletic games, which were a part of their celebrations. They used boxes to hold the collections; these were usually earthenware with a slot in the top for the coins.

With the coming of Christianity to Britain, it was common to find boxes in Churches at Christmas so that people could put money in them for the poor.

The day after Christmas was St. Stephen's Day, when the priests distributed the money among the needy, and so it became known as Boxing Day.

The Tramp

by Patricia Wingrave

**of the 1st Lutterworth Pack,
who wrote this poem for the Writer Badge**

It is dark in the wood,
Cold and still.
The wind is blowing,
The leaves are rustling,
I see a tramp curled up asleep;
The mice are playing in the warmth of his coat.
The mice awake him;
He is so sleepy.
I say "Hello" and hurry on.

The Queen on a "walk-about" during a visit to a city is cheered by children

To meet

Photograph by Miss W. J. Beer

Brown Owl had such exciting news for us in Pow-wow Ring.
She said, "The Queen herself will be coming in the spring.
A big reception is to be arranged in the Town Hall,
And they'll invite one Brownie Guide to represent us all.
I think this honour should be earned by someone who has tried
To show us what it really means to be a Brownie Guide."

I thought, with all my badges, she would choose me from the Pack,
And when she picked Jill Brown instead it took me quite aback,
For Jill comes in to meetings late, her dress and tie askew,
Her badges tacked on anyhow — with great big stitches, too!
When I reached home I cried and said that Brown Owl wasn't fair.
"That's not how Brownies are," I sobbed. "I was the best one there!"

the
Queen
by Sheila Deft

Then Mother took me on her knee. She didn't sympathise,
But what she said soon changed my mind and made me dry my eyes.
"Just think about your Promise, dear, and then you'll understand.
What matters most is not your dress but how you Lend a Hand.
You see, there are a lot of things Jill's mother cannot do,
Like threading needles, cutting bread, to mention only two.

"When Jill comes home from school each day, she helps," my mother said,
"To get the tea and clear away and put the twins to bed.
That's why she's late for Brownies, and those badges, you will find,
Have been stitched on by Jill herself — you see, her mother's blind!"
I felt ashamed to realise how selfish I had been,
For no one had a better right than Jill to meet the Queen.

Spider's Web

by L. M. Jones

Take out twelve pairs of words that go together, such as DRAGON and FLY (DRAGONFLY). What is left?

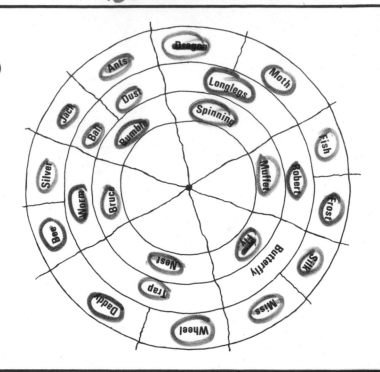

BUTTERFLY

Hidden Message

by Susan Leng

Fill in all the answers ACROSS. Then you will find a message to Brownies in the middle column DOWN

LEND A HAND

1. NEEDLE
2. TREFOIL
3. IRONING
4. TOADSTOOL
5. COMPASS
6. THRIFT
7. MESSAGE
8. VENTURE
9. GARDENER

1. You will need one of these for sewing.
2. The shape of the Brownie and Guide badges.
3. After the washing is dry, you could help with this.
4. Most Packs have one of these in the Brownie Ring.
5. This has a needle that always points to North.
6. There is a bee in this Brownie interest badge.
7. A Brownie learns to remember and deliver this.
8. This Brownie badge has a big V on it.
9. A wheelbarrow is on this badge.

mazes muddles

Message in Code

by Susan Leng

Can you read this semaphore message? Look up the semaphore alphabet in the *Brownie Guide Handbook* if you get stuck.

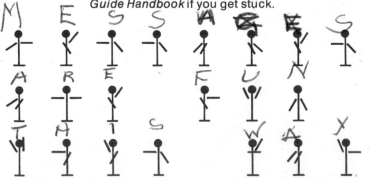

MESSAGE S
MARE E F U N
T H I S

Interest Badge Maze

by Daphne M. Pilcher

Can you find your way out of this maze? On the way you should spell out the names of five interest badges. You may move from one letter to the next letter up or down, to the left or right, but never diagonally. You pass through each letter once and only once on your way out.

C	R	T	P	I	D
R	A	F	O	R	E
E	T	S	N	Y	**END** R
R	J	E	**START** →	S	I
E	R	W	L	L	G
T	I	R	E	A	N

Brownie Maze Puzzle

by Daphne M. Pilcher

Can you show these Brownies the way through the maze to their Guider, Brown Owl?

The Road to the Revels

by Daphne M. Pilcher

Can you find it through the maze?

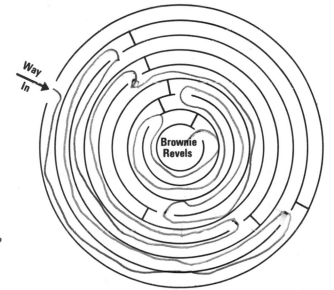

Way In →

Brownie Revels

and messages

FOR YOUR HALLOWE'EN PARTY

When your Pack has a Hallowe'en party, don't forget to decorate the Pack hall in a "witchy" way.

Put up pictures of black cats, witches and toads on the walls. You could find suitable pictures in magazines or paint them yourself. A large spider's web makes a striking decoration hung from the ceiling. This is easily made out of string.

How about baking witch-cakes? You could make these out of a gingerbread mixture and shape them to look like witches.

If you could borrow a large cooking-pot of the old-fashioned type, you could serve soup straight from the witches' cauldron. You will need a large quantity of packet-soup to fill the pot, but Brownies will enjoy the soup, especially if your Guider dresses up as a witch and serves it.
— L.B.

The Wizard's Birthday Party

by Aileen E. Passmore

At the wizard's party
  The strangest things occurred:
The teapot grew a pair of wings
  And sang just like a bird.
The cups and saucers danced a jig,
  And so did all the spoons,
Which on the silver fruit-dish
  Tinkled merry tunes.

The candles on the cake sent
  Up fountains of bright stars,
And from the wizard's larder
  Trooped all the big jam-jars;
They formed a guard of honour
  Around the wizard's chair;
A crock of apple-jelly cried,
  "A happy birthday, sir!"
The big cake grew enormous,
  And from a tiny door
Fairies, elves and pixies
  All began to pour.
They skipped across the table,
  And round the room they flew,
Singing "Happy birthday,
  Dear Wizard Wog, to you!"
It was the jolliest party
  For miles and miles around,
And all who'd been invited
  For days remained spellbound!

WISE WORDS

The only people you should get even with are those who have helped you.

Luck is a very good word — if you put the letter "P" before it.

When the head starts swelling, it means the mind's stopped growing.

Many a false step is made by standing still.

The only way to have a friend is to be a friend.

If you know what hurts you, you know what hurts others.

When at home — watch your temper. When in company — watch your tongue. When alone — watch your thoughts.

Look upon a New Year as a new adventure.

knotty problems

by Doris M. Hall

THE KNOTTIEST KNOT OF ALL

This is the round turn and two half-hitches

This is the *round-turn and two half-hitches*,
  Which I really think was invented by witches!
The spell laid upon it is baffling to me;
  I can't just describe how to tie it, you see!
But this I do know: 'tis a most useful knot—
  Almost as useful as any we've got.
'Twill hitch up a horse to a tethering-ring,
  Tie up the dog, or in parcelling string
Just at the place where a slip-knot is needed,
  You'll find that its usefulness can't be exceeded.
Now, I've told you *why*, but I can't describe *how*
  To tie this strange knot, so I'd best make my bow,
And leave it to Brown Owl or Tawny to teach,
  Since they can break any old witch-spell in reach!

SHEET-BEND MAGIC

You'll be well repaid for the time you may spend
  Upon learning just how to tie a *sheet-bend.*
It is used when you need to join *thin* rope to *thick*,
  Tie a rope to a loop, for it's both strong and quick.
You start with the thicker rope in the left hand;
  Turn back the end—make a loop—understand?
Imagine this loop to be quite a big hole,
  Nestling close up to a massive tree-bole.

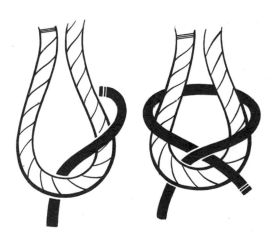

This is the way to tie a sheet-bend

Now in the right hand the thinner rope take
  (This one immediately turns into a snake!)
The "snake" peering up from its hole in the ground,
  Sees a tree standing, and takes a run round.
He runs just a little to quickly, alack,
  And gets caught 'neath his tail—on the way back!

*Now, don't you agree that knots are good fun?
And really most interesting once you've begun?*

How to See without being Seen

Anne Robertson Tells of the Clever Way Birds and Animals Use Camouflage

When you play stalking games during your outdoor meetings or on Pack holiday, you may hear the word "camouflage" said. Your Guider may tell you to make yourselves as hard to be seen as possible.

For example, if you are trying to hide amongst long grass and bracken, your Brownie uniform would make a good camouflage outfit, as it is brown and will blend in with the brown of the bracken and the green of the grass.

On the other hand, if you wish to hide on snow-covered ground, it would be best to wear white or cream.

Some of the best examples of camouflage can be found in the animal world. The Polar bear and Arctic fox are well coloured for concealment in snowy lands. Did you know that, in our own country, the ptarmigan and mountain-hare actually change their coats to suit the season? Both become white in winter, and turn back to brown in summer.

In the grasslands of Africa, the zebra and the giraffe are difficult to see against a background of sun and shadow, and the lion's sandy colour merges in with the parched grass and earth. The tiger of India is well hidden as he crouches in the jungle shadows ready to spring on his prey, his stripes resembling the streaks of shadow formed by the sunlight through twigs and branches.

Some members of the animal world disguise themselves in a very clever way. The stick-insect looks so much like the twigs he holds on to that you would have

The stick-insect looks very much like another twig on the branch

Photos by N.H.P.A.

Puzzle: find the woodcock, which sits on its nest and can hardly be distinguished from the foliage around

A chameleon, which is able to change colour to match its surroundings, and so protect itself from its enemies

great difficulty in finding him. You have probably heard tales too of the terror caused by crocodiles lying motionless in African rivers looking just like floating logs.

Did you know that even fish are camouflaged? The very young ones are transparent, and can hardly be seen in the water, and most others have dark upper-parts and silver under-parts so that their enemies above and below can't easily spot them.

You can perhaps think of some birds in our own country, such as the lark and grouse, which nest on open ground. These birds depend on their mottled brown plumage for concealment while nesting, and their eggs too are marked to resemble the pebbles and stones near by.

There is a strange reptile called a chameleon which actually changes its colour as it moves from one area to another!

War Camouflage

During the first and second world wars camouflage became very important to the army, navy and airforce services. A Camouflage Corps was formed and set to work to find ways of concealing men and weapons of war. One of the best-known forms of camouflage was of course the green and brown colouring of armaments, vehicles and buildings to make them look like their surroundings. Battle uniforms were in similar colours, and soldiers would sometimes cover their helmets with foliage when fighting in forest or jungle.

Very often armaments and buildings were covered with netting, and then leaves and branches would be added. Roads and factories were painted to look like greenery, and even dummy airfields were constructed to confuse enemy bombers. Snow troops wore white, and even tanks used in snowy conditions were painted white.

Next time you play a stalking game with your Pack, try to think of ways of camouflaging yourself and the other members of your Six. See, but don't be seen!

WHICH

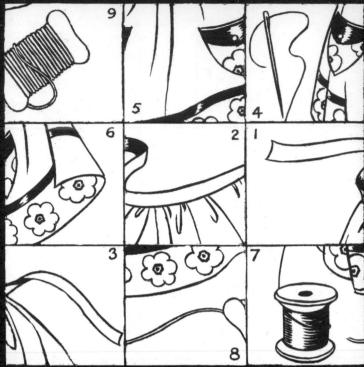

INTEREST

To find out which Brownie badge this picture represents, trace or copy the drawing in each frame into the one with the corresponding number in the blank frame. The completed picture will give you the clue to the interest badge.

BADGE?

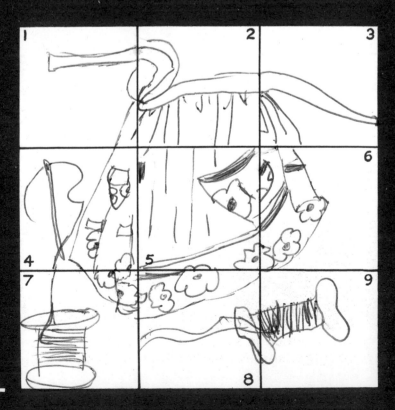

Brownies Make Things

Redhill (Surrey) Brownies make a garden in a plate
Photo by Mrs J. Tupper

Brownies lend a Hand

Brownies of the 160th Hillsborough Trinity Pack, Sheffield, lend a hand with the feet — by cleaning shoes.
Photo by Mrs Shirley Graves

brownies make things

by L. Baker

You will need play-dough or modelling-clay, straight spaghetti, black, white and brown poster-paint, two beads or dried peas, and a paintbrush.

a model hedgehog

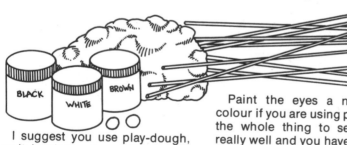

Paint the eyes a nice bright colour if you are using peas. Allow the whole thing to set and dry really well and you have an attractive model.

I suggest you use play-dough, as it hardens when left exposed to air for a while. Modelling-clay will do just as well.

Shape into an oval body with a pointed face, stick beads or peas in position to represent eyes.

Depending on the size of the hedgehog you are making, break or cut spaghetti into suitable lengths for spines.

Before setting your spines in clay, paint them with poster-paint. Hedgehog spines are white at base and banded black, white and brown all the way up, ending in a white tip.

your own

You require two empty washing-up liquid bottles, the large size, a little elastic, white enamel paint or fluorescent orange paint, a pair of scissors, and a paintbrush.

Measure a 7.5cm (3″) strip round the middle of each container. Draw a line all the way round. Paint the portion you have marked in enamel paint. Allow to dry overnight.

Cut off the top and bottom of the container around the lines you have marked. This should leave you with two tube-like pieces. Cut open up the side seam of each, and you will see

42

armbands

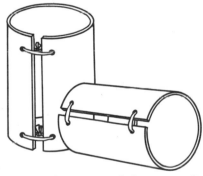

Daphne M. Pilcher
Explains How to Make It

a sweet basket

On the next page is a pattern for you to copy

that, being on a slight curve, it fits round your arm.

Depending on how big your arm is, you may need to attach elastic to the armbands at the top and bottom. Do this by making a hole and threading the elastic through it, securing it with a knot. The knot comes on the inside of the arm and so does not show.

When going to your Pack meeting in the dark, wear the armbands so that you will easily be seen by motorists.

Armbands are quite dear to buy in shops, so why not make sets and sell them for Pack funds?

It is nice when you give a present of sweets to put them in something attractive. This little basket is just the thing. It costs hardly anything, and it is easy to make.

You need some felt, enough to cut out the two shapes shown here (these are the actual size), and some embroidery thread or bright cotton. The only stitch you need to be able to sew is blanket-stitch.

First make two patterns of thin card, one of the basket and one of the handle. Place the patterns on your felt, draw round them, and

then carefully cut them out. Gather up each of the petals, pinning the side of A to the side of B, and so on all the way round till you have pinned the side of H to the other side of A. Fix the handle on parts A and E on the inside of the basket. Now you are ready to sew.

Blanket-stitch each petal on the *outside*, continuing round the top of each petal for decoration. Go round the handle too, to give it strength (see the drawing of the finished basket). Your basket is now ready for sweets, or you could use it for another gift such as bath-cubes.

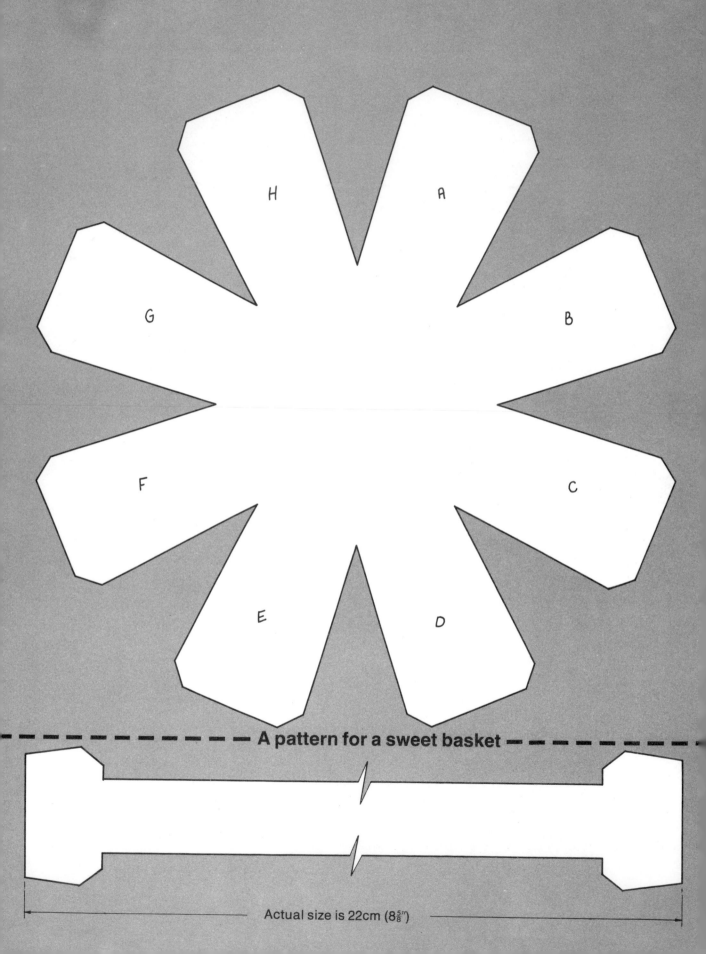

A pattern for a sweet basket

Actual size is 22cm ($8\frac{5}{8}$")

Erica's Easter Egg

by Jean Howard

Erica finished her breakfast and gave a big sigh. "Whatever is the matter?" asked her mother.

"Well, I don't want to be unkind, but why does Aunt Mary have to come and stay every Easter? She's so fussy; she spoils everything."

"What a horrid way to talk! When people live alone for most of the year it makes a change for them to have some cheerful company. Anyway, it looks like being a fine weekend, so you will be able to be outdoors most of the time. Perhaps some of your Six can come over and help you with the model and chart for the corner competition next term. Have you made a start on it yet?"

Erica sighed again. "No! I just can't think of anything original, and, anyway, everyone seems to be going away for Easter." She got up and helped to clear the table, looking far from her usual cheerful self.

Next day, about three o'clock, Aunt Mary arrived, and, sure enough, within half an hour she was saying that perhaps Erica would take the puppy into the garden as he was rather excitable and she had a new pair of stockings on. And Erica must be sure to shut the door as there was a draught.

After tea Erica wanted to watch her favourite TV programme, but Mother said Aunt Mary didn't care for television, and it might bring on one of her headaches.

So it was back to the garden again, where Erica cleaned and oiled her bicycle. She rode it up and down the lane, practising for the Road Safety Officer's test next term, when she would be allowed to ride to school, which was about a mile away from her father's farm.

She was quite glad to go to bed early. She read her *Brownie Annual* for a while; then, as she felt rather wide-awake, she decided to do the semaphore puzzle in it without looking up semaphore first in the *Brownie Guide Handbook*. After that she read a chapter of *The Wind in the Willows*, which was one of the books she had chosen to read for the Book Lover badge.

It was one of her favourite books, but that night everything seemed to get mixed up and she dreamed that Rat and Mole were having a bicycle race. As they rode madly down the lane with the puppy scampering behind, barking wildly, they turned the corner, and there was Aunt Mary standing in the middle of the road waving her umbrella and shouting, "Stop, stop! I command you to stop!"

Rat managed to pull up just in time, but when Mole applied his brakes nothing happened. On went the bike, helter-skelter, and then CRASH! Mole and puppy and Aunt Mary all ended up in a heap in the road—and Erica woke up.

Thank goodness it was only a dream! All the same, Erica determined to make sure her brakes were in good order before riding her bicycle again!

She looked at the clock. It was just after six, and Easter Sunday. Quietly she drew the curtains and saw that it was going to be a lovely day. Down on the farmyard the old cock was crowing, and the sound reminded her of the bag of Easter eggs in the drawer of her dressing-table, one for each member of the family.

Tipping them on to her bed, she began to put each one into a little nest of tissue-paper; then she took her crayons and some paper and made a tiny Easter card for each one. When they were all finished they looked very gay, and she put them ready to carry down to the breakfast table.

Suddenly an awful thought struck her. What about Aunt Mary? She had quite forgotten to buy one for her, and now it was too late. However tiresome Aunt Mary might be, she couldn't be left out.

Erica was wondering what to do when she heard the cock crow again and this gave her an idea. Dressing quickly, she crept downstairs and out of the back door. She hurried down to the barn where the hens roosted. They were prize Rhode Island Reds, and there in the first nesting-box was a beautiful large brown egg.

Erica wove a little nest and laid the egg in it

of the favourite homes of the brown furry caterpillar! We haven't time for that sort of thing now, though," she added, laughing.

As they hurried to catch up with the others, Erica said, "I think that's a splendid idea. Susan is a good artist and could do the pictures on the chart, and Mandy could do the printing; she's good at that sort of thing. The rest of us could do the model and help find specimens of flowers and insects. Will you come out after lunch and show me the best places to look?"

Aunt Mary nodded.

What an exciting afternoon it was! There was so much to discover, and Aunt Mary turned out to be a real naturalist.

They found speckled brown spiders in the bramblebushes and watched them swing on their slender threads, keeping a watchful eye for any unwary flies that might wander too near. A colony of ants trekked across a narrow path and went on a voyage of discovery up the bark of a sycamore

There was so much to discover. . . .

Picking up some wisps of straw, Erica wove a little nest and laid the egg in it. Yes, it looked fine! Back in the house, she made another Easter card to put in the nest, and all was well.

Changing out of her slacks, she put on her prettiest dress and brushed her hair till it shone; then she carried her Easter gifts downstairs and laid the breakfast table, placing a small nest on each plate and a bowl of primroses in the centre of the table.

An appetising smell of bacon came from the kitchen, and the household began to come down to breakfast. Aunt Mary was the last to arrive. Erica watched anxiously.

For a moment Aunt Mary just stood there smiling and holding the little nest in her hands. Then she took out the card and read, *A very happy Easter, Aunt Mary, with love from Erica.*

Somehow, Aunt Mary looked a changed person as she turned and said, "Thank you, Erica! What a very kind thought! I haven't had an Easter egg since I was a child,

and you've drawn me a very pretty card. What a lovely way to start Easter Day!"

Erica realised that Aunt Mary wasn't really so cross and difficult, after all. She lived alone, so was unused to the noise and bustle of family life. Erica gave her aunt a big hug and said, "I'm so glad you came to stay, Aunt Mary!"

At about half-past ten the family set out across the field for the old Norman church in the village. On the way Erica told Aunt Mary about the corner competition, and confessed that she couldn't think of a good idea for it. She'd been through the *Brownie Guide Handbook*, but nothing suitable came to her mind.

Aunt Mary thought for a moment, and then she said, "What about something to do with the out-of-doors? You could make a model of a field, with hedges and paths and a gate, and then show on a chart the sort of wildflowers and insects and other small creatures that would be found there. Look, here is some ragwort, which is one

. . . a baby frog jumped out of the ditch. . . .

46

tree. Further along, the track led up to a five-bar gate where cattle had churned up the ground into a sea of mud. Lifting a large stone by the gatepost, they found a family of woodlice, who rolled up into tight little balls or went scattering in all directions. A snail's shell lay on a brick where a bird had dropped it to smash the shell so that it could pick out a tasty morsel for its breakfast, and several fat brown slugs made incredibly slow progress through the wet grass by a ditch, which was full of water after some recent heavy rain.

They were standing watching the slugs when a baby frog jumped out of the ditch and nearly landed on Erica's foot. She laughed as it leapt away and hid in a clump of wild parsley, and said she wasn't sure who had had the worst fright. Ladybirds made tiny spots of colour on a bush of broom, and it was so warm that even a few early butterflies were trying out their wings. In the long tangled grass by the hedge a family of fieldmice were trying to keep well hidden from the sharp eyes of their enemy the hawk.

Erica had a wonderful time, and could hardly wait to tell her Six about the idea. Even if they didn't win the competition they would learn a lot about Nature's wonderful ways.

That evening Erica heard her aunt saying she hadn't spent such an enjoyable afternoon for ages, and when Mother came in to say goodnight Erica said, "I'm sorry I was so horrid about Aunt Mary coming to stay. I think she's quite super and I hope she will come again in the summer. We could all go on a Nature trail with her and work for the Discoverer badge. It's much more fun going with someone who knows what to look for."

This was the beginning of many hours of enjoyment for Erica and her Six. About a year later Aunt Mary moved to a little cottage in the village, where Brownies were always welcome and where Erica saw to it that Aunt Mary was never lonely.

And it had all begun with an Easter egg!

Easter Table Decoration

For this attractive Easter decoration you will need thin card, paints or crayons, gummed tape or glue, and scissors.

Draw a row of Easter designs on your card, like those in the drawing.

Cut out these designs, but leave them attached to the base strip, which should be about 25.5cm (10") long. Colour the designs on both sides. Bend the strip round, and fix with glue or gummed tape.

You could make three or four of these to stand on the tea-table at Easter.

Glue Here

by Anne Robertson

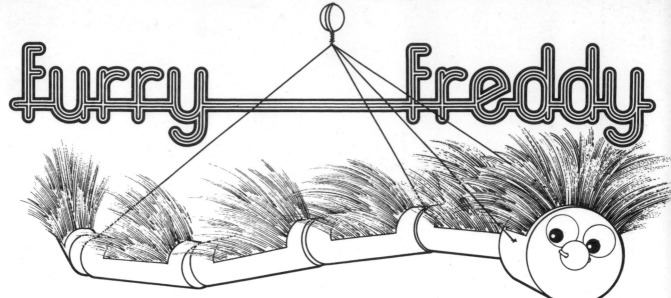

Furry Freddy

Furry Freddy is 28cm (11") long. To make him, you need five empty cotton-spools of the narrow kind, one large empty cotton-reel, black felt 18cm (7") by 15cm (6"), scraps of long-haired fur fabric, 61cm (24") of black hat elastic, two wooden beads, two moveable "eyes", and thread.

Cut two circles of black felt as pattern A and one rectangle as pattern B. With these cover the large cotton-reel, oversewing the seams.

Cut ten circles of black felt as pattern C and five squares as pattern D and use them to cover the narrow spools. Cut a hole in the centre of each circle to match the centre hole of each spool.

Sew a scrap of fur fabric on the top of each covered spool.

Thread one bead on to the elastic; double over so that the bead is in the centre, and thread the ends through the large cotton-reel, then through each of the smaller spools. Thread one end of the elastic through the second bead. Tie the ends of the elastic together, pushing the knot inside the last spool.

Sew moveable "eyes" in place on the large cotton-reel. If you can't get "eyes", use circles of felt instead. Omit the "eyes" if for a baby brother or sister.

Cut two pieces of black thread about 61cm (24") long. Fasten the first to each side of the large cotton-reel and the second between the first and second and fourth and fifth narrow spools.

B.M. Carr Shows You How to Make a Charming Caterpillar Puppet

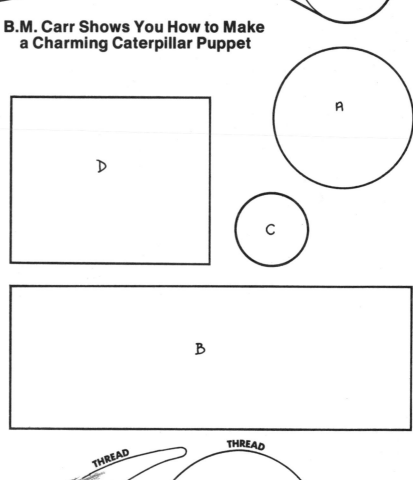

48

a NEW BIKE for you and £50 for your PACK

Yes, that is the wonderful double prize you could win by entering this simple competition.

All you have to do is to pick out which you think is the best and the next-best story, article, poem, how-to-make, and puzzle in the five groups listed on this page.

The Editor has made his choice. Each BEST that agrees with his will gain five points, each NEXT BEST three points. The competitor with the highest number of points will win the grand double prize.

GROUP 1: *STORIES*
A Pack Holiday Adventure
B Brownies in the Enchanted Wood
C Erica's Easter Egg
D Heather and the Baby-Next-Door
E The Pathfinders

GROUP 2: *ARTICLES*
A Who Was Miss Muffet?
B See Without Being Seen
C My Animal Friends
D The Rescue of Bambi
E Do You Believe in Fairies?
F Calling All Signallers

GROUP 3: *POEMS*
A Brownie Prayer
B To Meet the Queen
C The Wizard's Birthday Party
D Brownie Song

GROUP 4: *MAKING THINGS*
A Garden Picture
B Sweet Basket
C Furry Freddy
D For Your Hallowe'en Party
E Easter Gifts
F Models From Odds and Ends
G Matchbox Horse

GROUP 5: PUZZLES
A Which Six Reach Toadstool?
B Brownies of Other Lands
C Island of Flowers
D Road to the Revels
E Interest Badge Maze
F Name the Birds
G Hidden Message
H Brownie Maze
I Find the Animals
J Flower Puzzle
K Picture Crossword

THE BROWNIE ANNUAL 1977
COMPETITION ENTRY FORM

Just write down the letter that is set against the title of your choice in each of the groups listed on this page.

GROUP 1 *STORIES*	BEST_____ NEXT BEST_____	My name is.. My address is..
GROUP 2 *ARTICLES*	BEST _____ NEXT BEST_____	....My age is...........
GROUP 3 *POEMS*	BEST_____ NEXT BEST_____	My Pack is.. ....
GROUP 4 *MAKING THINGS*	BEST_____ NEXT BEST_____	My Guider's name and address is...................
GROUP 5 *PUZZLES*	BEST_____ NEXT BEST_____	....

GRAND

DOUBLE-

PRIZE

COMPETITION

Enter this simple and interesting competition and give yourself the chance of winning a brand-new bicycle for yourself and £50 for your Pack.

The competition gives every Brownie, regardless of age, an equal chance.

When you have chosen your BEST and NEXT-BEST contributions, write down in not more than about fifty words what you like most about the *Brownie Annual* — its pictures, its stories, its puzzles or poems, the information it gives you or the way it sets you thinking about things to do or to make — perhaps the laughs it gives you!

Your little write-up will be taken into account if there should be competitors with the same number of winning points.

If you win and would rather have something else of equal value to a bicycle you may do so.

Complete front and back of the entry form and post it to THE BROWNIE ANNUAL 1977 COMPETITION, PURNELL BOOKS, BERKSHIRE HOUSE, QUEEN STREET, MAIDENHEAD, BERKSHIRE, SL6 1NF, to arrive not later than March 31st, 1977. The winner will be notified and the prize awarded as soon after this date as possible.

The publishers' decision is final, and no correspondence will be entered into in connection with the competition.

What I like most about the Brownie Annual

Photo by Robert Moss

Emma's Prize Playmate

Emma's mother was looking after a friend's dog, whose name was Jake and who was a Rotweiner bullhound, a most unusual breed. Emma and Jake became friends and playmates. Jake was big and Emma was small, so they were about the same size!

One day, just before leaving for Pack meeting, Emma took Jake for a walk in the park, where a dog show was being held. There was a notice on a gate inviting children to enter their dogs in competitions for THE PRETTIEST DOG, THE DOG MOST LIKE ITS OWNER, THE DOG WITH THE LOUDEST BARK, AND THE MOST UNUSUAL DOG.

"Well," said Emma to Jake, "Mummy said you were a most unusual dog, so I think you ought to go in for this competition."

She ran home and told her mother, who agreed that Jake should enter THE MOST UNUSUAL DOG class.

And Jake won! He was awarded a juicy bone, and Emma a bar of chocolate. Emma was delighted. So was Jake—but more with the bone!

Emma and her playmate, Jake

51

NIGHT ALARM

AN EXCITING GUIDE CAMP ADVENTURE IN PICTURES

Adapted by Robert Moss

THAT NIGHT.....

I'M SURE I SHALL SLEEP LIKE THE LOGS WE'VE BEEN GATHERING!

IF I DON'T DREAM OF ENDLESS STACKS OF WOOD I SHALL BE RUN DOWN BY GALLOPING HORSES

THANK GOODNESS THERE AREN'T ANY COWS IN OUR FIELD. I'M SCARED OF COWS

HILARY! WAKE UP, HILARY! THERE'S SOMEBODY OUTSIDE THE TENT

YOU MUST HAVE BEEN HAVING THE DREAM BECKY EXPECTED, RUTH

I TELL YOU THE TENT BULGED, HILARY, AS IF SOMETHING WAS TRYING TO GET IN

NEXT DAY BARBARA PREECE VISITED THE GUIDE CAMP WITH HER FATHER

MAJOR PREECE'S DAUGHTER WANTS YOU TO KEEP YOUR EYES OPEN FOR HER PONY, SULTAN, WHICH SOMEHOW GOT OUT OF HIS PADDOCK LAST NIGHT AND CAN'T BE FOUND. PLEASE REPORT TO ME IF YOU SEE A PONY WANDERING ABOUT. THE PONY IS QUIET AND DOCILE, SO YOU NEEDN'T BE AFRAID OF IT

RUTH HEARD SOMETHING OUTSIDE OUR TENT LAST NIGHT. SHE WOKE ME UP, BUT I THOUGHT SHE'D DREAMED IT

SOMETHING PUSHED AGAINST THE TENT AND MADE IT BULGE

YOU HEARD MY GENTLE PONY OUTSIDE YOUR TENT AND WERE TOO SCARED TO GO OUT TO HIM! AND GUIDES ARE SUPPOSED TO HAVE COURAGE! I MAY NEVER SEE SULTAN AGAIN NOW, BECAUSE YOU HADN'T THE SPIRIT TO GO OUTSIDE YOUR TENT IN THE DARK

53

January has the snowdrop for its special flower, although most snowdrops do not bloom until February. The snowdrop brightens the winter scene for us. The poet Rossetti wrote about snowdrops that when all earth seems gripped in frosty silence they "prove the world awake".

February has the primrose, but it is only the very first primroses that appear so early. The word primrose means "first rose", although it is nothing like a rose.

It is a charming flower, and gives one of the first hints of spring.

March has the violet for its flower. The name violet is a very old one and its meaning is forgotten. Some wild violets found in the woods and hedgerows have scent, and these are called sweet violets. Wild ones without a scent are called dog violets.

April's flower is the daisy, which means "eye of the day". Today we call big daisies marguerites, but this used to mean little daisies as well. The word means "pearl", perhaps because the daisy chain made by children looks rather like a chain of pearls.

Photographs by Miss W. J. Beer

May: You will easily guess what the special flower of this lovely month is. It is the hawthorn, from which the may blossom scents and beautifies the world with delightful fragrance and colour. As the poet wrote: "May makes the heart feel gay."

June, a month of many flowers, has the honeysuckle. This used to be called simply honey-suck, because children, like the bees, loved to suck honey from the sweet-smelling flower. The honeysuckle makes a lovely garland on the summer hedgerows.

birthday flower?

September has morning glory for its flower. Another name for this pretty blue flower is the moon creeper. The reason for this curious name is that it flowers only in the early morning, fading by noon. It belongs to the convolvulus family.

October has the hop, with its catkins, for its flower. It grows on long stalks and is of the same family as the hops used for beer-making. The hop flower is red and looks as if it is made of crinkly dry paper.

...ly has the water-lily. In ...cient times people thought ...at a nymph, a kind of fairy, ...ed to haunt the water-lily. ... if your birthday month is ...ly you must share your ...wer with the fairies. There's ...ovely thought for you!

Photographs by Mrs D. H. Blowers

Each month has its special flower. Sometimes the flower is only just beginning to appear, but perhaps it is named the flower of that month because it is the first or even the only flower to bloom.

November's flower is the chrysanthemum, which means "gold flower". The chrysanthemum was brought from Japan and China, where the summers are shorter than they are here. That is why it flowers in this country when the days are shorter—and how welcome it is!

August has the poppy, "fire in the cornfields". People used to call the poppy "headache", their quaint belief being that its strong smell produced a headache! A poet wrote: "Come poppies that in crimson dwell, called headaches from their sickly smell."

December gives us the holly, which decorates our homes at Christmastime. Children used to say that the prickly-leaved holly was a "boy" and the smooth-leaved holly a "girl", and they would try to collect bunches of "boys and girls".

Peeling potatoes

Photo: John Warburton

Pack Holidays

by Ailsa Brambleby

Have you ever thought what fun it would be to have a house of your own to look after, even if it were only for a few days? Well, that's what happens if you go on a Pack holiday like the Brownies in the photographs.

Pack holidays are special Brownie holidays. The Pack borrow a building and set up house there for about a week. All kinds of queer places have been used for Pack holidays, including schools, church halls, large bungalows, and country cottages. One Pack has even had a kind of old theatre, and each night Pack Leader had to climb up on to the stage to go to bed! Some lucky Brownies have had holidays in the special Pack holiday houses that belong to the Movement; these are in the grounds of Waddow Hall (Lancashire),

Play on Pack holiday

Photo: Church Army

Netherurd (Scotland), and Bron-eirion (Wales). Perhaps your Guider will tell you about them.

Once you reach your Pack holiday house you may find you are no longer a Gnome or Kelpie or whatever Six you normally are, for very often the Pack chooses new names from favourite books. One group I know took their names from *Peter Pan*. The Brownie Guider became Peter, the First Aider of course became Nana, and as Pack Leader's own name was Wendy she kept to it! The Sixes became Red Indians, Lost Boys and Mermaids, and all wore beautifully embroidered emblems for these characters.

There's plenty of work and

Bed-making
Photo: Don Reed Studios

Rest hour
Photo: Don Reed Studios

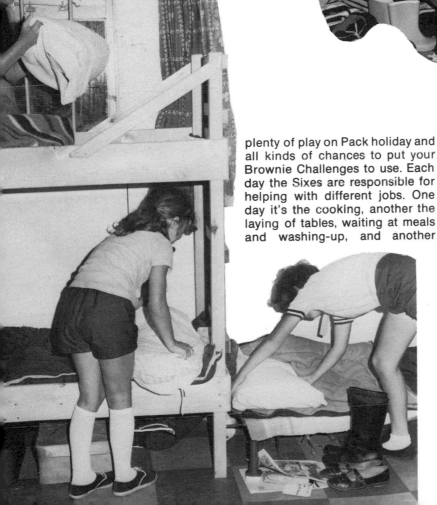

plenty of play on Pack holiday and all kinds of chances to put your Brownie Challenges to use. Each day the Sixes are responsible for helping with different jobs. One day it's the cooking, another the laying of tables, waiting at meals and washing-up, and another

keeping the house clean. Then, of course, there's the post to collect, flowers to arrange, shoes and badges to clean, and visitors to welcome and look after. In spare time there are all kinds of exciting things to do, such as treasure hunts, nature challenges, secret good turns, bathing, and picnics.

All kinds of problems and surprises may crop up when you are on Pack holiday (we once had a flood and had to move all the beds out of the dormitory!), but Brownies soon learn to find a way out of every difficulty. They also learn to look after themselves *and* to think of other people as well. So you can easily see that Brownies who have been on Pack holiday often make very good campers when they become Guides.

59

"I'm so sorry I'm late, Brown Owl," gasped Heather, almost throwing herself into the Church Hall, where the weekly meeting had just begun, "but I was minding the baby-next-door."

"Steady, steady!" said Mrs Rhodes, the Brownie Guider, calmly. "Now come and sit down quietly. We're about to have a Pow-wow to discuss a new Pack Venture."

Heather settled herself down with the rest of the Elf Six between her friends Jane and Frances.

"The baby-next-door has cut another tooth," she whispered.

"Oh, you and that baby-next-door!" muttered Jane.

"Sshh!" hissed the other girls as Mrs Rhodes began to speak.

"There is a new Pack Venture that Anne Merton suggested last week. I should like to discuss it," she said. "The idea is for a sale of work to raise money to help the deaf children. There would be lots to do, but it's a chance for everyone of us to do something to help. Whatever you are best at you could do. You have all been working hard at badgework recently, and I know we have some very good needlewomen and cooks among us."

All the Brownies thought a sale of work a splendid idea and were soon buzzing with good suggestions. Someone offered to make aprons, and another cushion-covers. Jane said she'd bake cakes for the cake-stall. Frances remembered the toys she had made for the Toymaker badge and promised to make several more. Little Susan, the newest recruit,

**Heather settled herself
down with the rest of the Elf Six**

decided that she would make book-markers. There was no end to the suggestions—from everyone except Heather. Heather had never been very good at anything in particular. She never stopped trying; in fact, she probably tried harder than most; but things never turned out quite as well as she intended they should.

"To begin with," Mrs Rhodes announced, "we shall have a poster competition. You can all make posters to advertise the sale, and there will be a small prize for the best one."

After Pow-wow, for the rest of the meeting, Heather dismissed the subject from her mind, but on the way home she began to think hard about it.

None of the other Brownies came her way. There were only two little white cottages at the end of the lane. In one of these lived Heather and her parents. She had been lonely at one time, as both her brother and sister were already grown up and had left home, but now that the new family had moved in next door (a mother, a father and a chubby little baby girl who had just learnt to crawl about the floor) things were a lot better. Heather loved babies and especially this jolly little one, who was named Rosemary but was more usually called "Rolly-Romy", so it was not surprising that she spent a lot of her time amusing the baby.

Now, thinking about the sale of

and the
xt-Door

by Ann Rogers

"I must do better next time"

work, Heather decided that she'd first better try to make a nice poster. She began that evening. A great amount of care went into painting the words in bright-red and decorating the border with balloons in every colour that her paintbox held. She was quite proud of the result, and took the poster along to the next Pack meeting, when the competition was to be judged. Hoots of laughter greeted it. It read:

> BROWNIE
>
> SAIL OF WERK
>
> IN CHERCH HALL ON
>
> SATADAY NOVMBER 9TH
>
> 3 O'CLOK
>
> IN ADE OF DEF CHILDRUN

"Oh, Heather!" laughed Mrs Rhodes. "It's a beautiful poster, and I can see that you have put a lot of work into it, but the spell-ing! It's terrible! You should have checked it first. I don't think we can put it up like that. Perhaps you'd do better at making things to sell."

Heather was disappointed, but cheered up when her friend Frances, the Elf Second, won the prize.

"I must do better next time," she muttered to herself as once again she trudged homewards, head bowed against the autumn winds, "but what shall I do? Bake cakes?" No! She remembered that the fairy cakes she had attempted for the Cook badge were far from fairylike. The sausages and bread she fried had been quite delicious, but they were not the sort of things that could be put on a cake-stall! "But I could make some sand-wiches for the teas!" She brighten-ed at this thought, but it was not enough, she decided. She would have to try doing some needle-work.

She still hadn't decided what to make when she fetched her needle-work basket. This contained a bundle of wools, silks and tangled reels of cotton. She began to sort it out. In doing so she discovered eight empty cotton-reels and two more with only a twist of thread left on them. To be tidy, she slipped the reels onto an odd length of string—and then had a bright idea! The string of reels looked

Sammy Serpent

like a snake. Painted, it would make a lovely toy for a small child. Yes, a ball would make it a splendid head! There was a bald tennis-ball at the back of the toy cupboard. That would do.

The idea excited her and she rushed out into the kitchen to tell her mother, who thought it a lovely

Rosemary clutched at it at once

idea and offered to make the holes in the ball for threading and also suggested a cork for its nose and another for the tip of its tail.

Heather found some lacquer and began painting the ball, reels and corks, so that Sammy Serpent, as she called him, had a blue body

with red spots and squiggles along it, strange yellow-and-green eyes and a red nose. When the pieces were dry she threaded them back onto the string, with a knot at each end to stop them from slipping and a lot of string left over so that a little child could pull him along.

She was so pleased with the result that she took it next door straight away to see if the baby, Rosemary, liked it too. Rosemary clutched at it at once.

"How kind of you!" said Rosemary's mother. "You are clever, too, to make Rosemary such a nice toy."

Heather opened her mouth to explain that the toy was really for the Brownie sale of work, but she couldn't take the toy from the baby now.

Instead she said: "It's nothing, really. I'm glad she likes it." Then, "Will you be coming to our Brownie sale on Saturday, Mrs Jones?"

"I should like to come," Rosemary's mother replied, "but it's difficult really. I have no one to mind Rosemary, and it would be too awkward taking a push-chair round the crowded Church Hall. I'd be banging people's legs all the time, and Rosemary is certainly too heavy for me to carry for long. I'll come next year, when Rosemary will be able to walk by herself."

"Well, no one can say I don't try," thought Heather as she went back to her own house. "I suppose I'll just have to make an extra lot of sandwiches for the tea-stall now."

It was then that she had her second bright idea of the day. At the same time, Mrs Jones came to the back door and called for her.

"I've found this bag of old cotton-reels," she explained. "I thought perhaps you might like to make another Sammy Serpent, like Rosemary's, for the Brownie sale."

Heather had to smile at that, but she began work with renewed enthusiasm.

At the next Pack meeting Mrs Rhodes saw Sammy-Serpent-the-Second and was delighted with it. She liked Heather's other idea too —a nursery corner at the sale. She asked Heather to copy the words "Babies Minded" carefully on the bottom of all the posters on display. Then the Elves were given the task of organising the nursery corner.

The Brownies lent toys, including even a small rocking horse, and throughout the sale looked after babies and toddlers so that the mothers could wander about the stalls and sit and chat at the tea corner without having to worry about their small children, and the small children played happily with the Elves without having to worry about their mothers! They all had fun.

Mrs Jones and Rosemary and other mothers with small children were able to come because of Heather's idea, and the sale was a great success. The Brownies raised a lot of money to help buy special equipment to aid deaf children in their lessons, and, as Mrs Rhodes said at the beginning, it had been a Venture in which everyone could do whatever they were best at. Everyone enjoyed it too—especially Heather and the Baby-Next-Door!

The Brownie sale

the Rescue of Bambi

by Lewis Lyon

This is a true story of the rescue by a kind family of an orphaned baby deer

It was evening time in early summer, and Mr Basil Davies was enjoying a stroll near his home, set among the rolling Quantock Hills in Somerset. Suddenly, viciously, from the woodland about half a mile away, came the reports of two gunshots in rapid succession. Mr Davies wondered whether a local farmer was out shooting rabbits or woodpigeons and so resumed his walk.

But four days later he realised what those two gunshots meant. On a Sunday-afternoon walk he came across a very weak and exhausted baby deer, which tottered unsteadily towards him, bleating for milk. He now realised, all too well, that it had been a poacher's gun that fired those two shots, which had undoubtedly killed the mother deer.

In consequence, the little calf (as red deer young are called) had been without its mother's milk for four days. His strong but gentle hands lifted up the helpless creature and carried it to the shelter of his cottage. There, a baby's feeding bottle was soon filled and put into effective action. Operation Deer Rescue was under way!

Mr. Davies, whose work happened to be concerned with deer and who knew quite a bit about them, judged the orphan's age to be about six weeks. After an anxious time at first, "Bambi", as his family called her, began to recover her strength and to make good progress, responding well to the care and attention lavished upon her. As the weeks went by, she grew into a healthy and active animal and became very affectionate towards her foster parents.

But, having saved her life, they were now faced with the awkward question, "What are we going to do with her?" They couldn't just release her into the woodland, for, without her mother's protection, she would certainly not be able to fend for herself and might easily become a prey for a fox. Their own garden space was limited, and a young and active red deer calf could not be relied upon to show much respect for their garden produce! It would be unthinkable to tether her. What was needed was an exercise paddock. In this difficult situation a welcome visitor arrived on the scene; one who was to provide a solution to the problem. He was Mr David Percy, who took a great interest in deer and was, in fact, Chairman of the Wessex Branch of the Deer Society. He had plenty of space in the garden of his Brockenhurst home, and his young twin daughters, Heather and Margaret, would be delighted to look after "Bambi".

Arrangements were soon made for the now four-month-old deer-calf to be transported one hundred miles by road from the Quantocks to the New Forest. A specially pre-pared straw-lined crate was provided.

With the precious cargo safely aboard his trailer, Mr Percy made the journey in about three and a half hours, much to the delight of his twin daughters. Re-christened "Corrie", the young deer soon adapted to her new surroundings and thrived under the devoted care of the Percy family. Even their dog, "Jessie", proved to be friendly and showed no resentment towards the latest addition to the family.

But on Boxing Day, there was consternation in the household. Corrie was missing from her paddock! For hours, Mr Percy and his daughters searched and called for her in the forest, but without result. The girls, close to tears, were feeling utterly wretched. What *could* have happened to her? Then, at about noon, a forest keeper brought welcome news. Their lost pet had turned up at the meet of the New Forest Foxhounds on Balmer Lawn! There, she had made new friends, who were amazed to come across so

"Take a good look at me—don't you think I've got a fine pair of ears?"

"This is a back view of me—hope you like it"

"This is one of my Cub Scout friends, Paul Radford. He wants to pat me, but I'd rather have something to eat"

Colour prints by W. L. Westcott

"The dog's my friend Jess, but I'm not speaking to him this morning"

A—E

65

tame a young red deer in the New Forest. Corrie was enjoying her new popularity!

She was soon re-united with the Percy family, who were very relieved to get her safely back after her adventurous "coming out" into society. The paddock fencing was repaired, and there were no further causes for alarm.

The Percy family later moved to Malvern, and Corrie took up residence among a herd of red deer on the Eastnor Castle estate, not far from Malvern, once the home of Lord Somers, a former Chief Scout, and now the residence of Major Harvey-Bathurst and his wife, Lord Somers' daughter. The Percys are able to keep in close touch with Corrie in her new home.

Corrie is no longer a baby deer. She is growing up. Not only is she in splendid condition, but she is a contented animal. The fact that she is reflects much credit on the patience, kindness and understanding of all those good friends who helped in "Operation Deer Rescue".

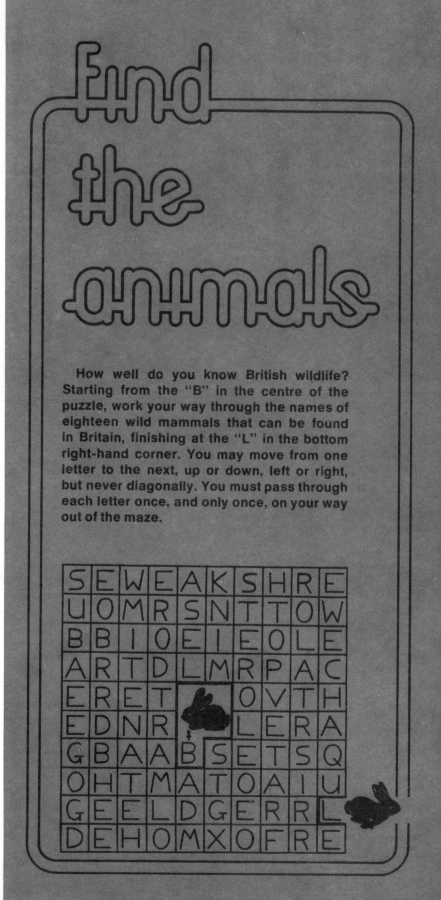

Find the animals

How well do you know British wildlife? Starting from the "B" in the centre of the puzzle, work your way through the names of eighteen wild mammals that can be found in Britain, finishing at the "L" in the bottom right-hand corner. You may move from one letter to the next, up or down, left or right, but never diagonally. You must pass through each letter once, and only once, on your way out of the maze.

S	E	W	E	A	K	S	H	R	E
U	O	M	R	S	N	T	T	O	W
B	B	I	O	E	I	E	O	L	E
A	R	T	D	L	M	R	P	A	C
E	R	E	T			O	V	T	H
E	D	N	R			L	E	R	A
G	B	A	A	B	S	E	T	S	Q
O	H	T	M	A	T	O	A	I	U
G	E	E	L	D	G	E	R	R	L
D	E	H	O	M	X	O	F	R	E

Easter Gifts to Make

by P. M. E. Knight

For **Ronny Rabbit** you will need a bath cube, a piece of coloured crepe paper about 18cm (7″) by 13cm (5″), ribbon, tissue-paper, scraps of coloured paper, and cotton.

Place the bath-cube in the centre of the crepe paper. Fold in the sides of the paper and tie tightly with cotton at the top.

Roll the tissue-paper into a ball for the head. Place it inside the crepe paper on top of the bath-cube, and tie tightly at the top with cotton. Divide the length left at the top into two and shape as ears.

With bits of coloured paper, stick on shapes for eyes and mouth. Finally, tie a ribbon bow round the "neck".

For an **Easter Egg** you will need part of an egg carton, an empty eggshell washed and dried, foil, coloured crepe paper, a few small sweets, a piece of narrow ribbon, and a piece of cling-wrap.

Cut a portion from the bottom of an egg-carton. Cover it with crepe paper. Carefully cover the eggshell with foil. Place it in the carton. Fill the shell with small sweets. Cover the whole with cling-wrap, and tie a bow round the centre.

Now you have an attractive Easter-egg gift.

The rope-bridge is the top attraction at Gloucestershire's Open Day at Cowley Deer Park

Colour slide by Robert Moss

On Pack holiday at Dinedor Adventure Centre, near Hereford, these 1st Eastnor Brownies shelter under groundsheets while their supper sausages cook

Colour slide by Miss J. Bursnell

Brownies of the 1st Eastnor Pack set off to work for the Discoverer badge

Colour slide by Miss J. Bursnell

wnie Revels and Holidays

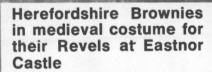

This balloon girl belongs to the 24th York (Dinghouses) Pack
Colour slide by Mrs J. Fisher

Herefordshire Brownies in medieval costume for their Revels at Eastnor Castle
Colour slide by Robert Moss

West Indian Brownies of the 86th Leeds (St. Martin's) Pack enjoy "elevenses" during Pack holiday
Colour slide by Mrs A. Lockyear

will it be Sunny

by Trevor Holloway

or

Nature always sends advance news of tomorrow's weather. The clouds, the tints of the sky, the behaviour of birds and insects, all provide clues.

What are the clues to look for, and what kind of weather do they foretell? Do you know?

Even if you live in a town or city, you can keep an eye on the clouds. If you see fluffy white clouds like masses of cotton-wool drifting across the sky, fine (and probably warm) weather may be

expected. These clouds are called cumulus clouds.

Another cheery cloud is the type that makes what is often called a "mackerel" sky. This cloud formation is made up of hundreds of tiny cloudlets which look like the scales of a fish. If you see these clouds you will know that warmer and more settled weather is on the way.

Cirrus clouds are the kind sometimes called "mares' tails"—whispy streaks of white like the tail of a white horse. They usually foretell strong wind.

Have you ever seen a "rainbow" around the moon? If the corona, as it is called, grows in diameter, you will need your raincoat tomorrow; if it becomes smaller the risk of rain the following day is very slight.

Fir-cones close their "petals"

Cumulus clouds

A mackerel sky

when rain is on the way and open them wide when fine weather is coming. A bunch of dried teasel-heads will behave in the same way, too.

The tints of the sky soon after dawn can tell the weather-watcher much. A pink dawn sky means blustery winds and maybe a few showers; if the sky has a greenish-yellow tint, it's almost certain to be a rainy day—probably with very heavy rain. A beautiful crimson sunset, as you are sure to know, is promise of a lovely day on the morrow.

Birds can sense a coming storm long before we can. They stop singing and retire to the shelter of trees and bushes, where you may see them preening their feathers. Country folk say they are putting on their raincoats!

Spiders are expert weather-prophets. If, in the early morning, you see their gossamer threads trailing over grass and hedgerows, or if you feel cobweb clinging to

your face as you pass between bushes, a fine day is certain. The experts tell us that spiders always know when it is safe for them to wander further afield than usual. Beekeepers will also tell you that bees fly much farther from the hive in search of pollen when the outlook is good.

When you can see trees and other objects on the distant horizon standing out bolder and clearer than usual, you may be sure that rain is not far away.

If you live in the country you may have noticed that cattle lie down in the fields before a storm. The farmers say that this is because they know it's going to rain and are taking care to have at least one dry spot to lie on! But don't place any faith in the old saying that if a cat washes behind its ears it's going to rain. Cats—dainty creatures that they are—wash behind their ears *every* day, even in the middle of a heat-wave!

grow a bean

Brenda Morton Shows You How

Put blotting-paper round the inside of a jamjar and sand in the bottom. Slip a broad bean between the blotting-paper and the glass about halfway down.

Keep the sand damp and watch your bean grow. When the stalk comes above the jar, plant the bean in the garden.

bean

sand

Name the Birds

by A. L. Blowers

How many of these birds do you know?

7. My home is high on a cliff, but you may see me at the Tower of London

8. I live by the sea and dive for my m— of fish

4. I'm a bird of prey of the falcon family

1. I'm one of Britain's smallest birds

2. I'm a night-bird seldom seen by day

5. Even if I have a harsh voice, I'm handsome

9. You see and hear me lanes and hedgerows

3. I swoop and soar at speed through the air

6. I sing at night as well as by day

10. I'm the bird of peac—

15. I live on the moors

19. I'm a fast flyer

18. I'm a friendly, chirpy fellow and I like being on Christmas cards

11. I take my name from my tail

People love to listen to my song

16. I'm the terror of small birds

20. I'm black all over, and my voice is a croak

I'm big and black and my voice is a croak

17. The black patch on my head gives me my name

21. My throat gives me my name

I'm sometimes called the king of British birds

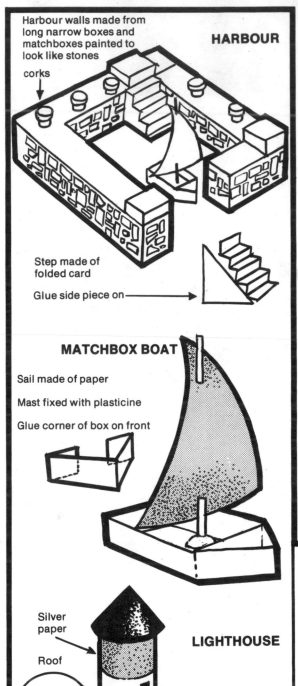

HARBOUR

Harbour walls made from long narrow boxes and matchboxes painted to look like stones

corks

Step made of folded card

Glue side piece on ⟶

brownies make things

Anne Robertson Suggests Some Simple Models for You to Make from Odds and Ends

Look round your house *now* and see if you can find any throw-away odds and ends which could be put together, and, with a coat of paint added, made into interesting or amusing models.

You should be able to find the following fairly easily: old cotton-reels, plastic bottles, cardboard, paper, matchboxes, used matches, wool, thread, cloth, shoeboxes and string. In addition to these you will probably need glue, gummed tape, scissors, a ruler, a pencil, paint and plasticine.

MATCHBOX BOAT

Sail made of paper

Mast fixed with plasticine

Glue corner of box on front

LIGHTHOUSE

Silver paper

Roof

Tube of cardboard

For roof, bend into cone shape and fix with glue

Paint door and windows on

WINDMILL

Plastic bottle

Sails of stiff card fixed at centre with paper-fastener

Steps are strips of card with matchsticks glued on

Draw lines on sails

SNOWMAN

Paper hat

Ribbon scarf

Eyes, gloves, buttons of paper

Plastic bottle for body

Cotton-wool

CLOCK

Cardboard face

Moveable hands fixed at centre with paper-fastener

Having collected as many of these items as possible, your next problem is to decide what to make. Perhaps the scrap materials will suggest a shape to you. Perhaps you have gained some ideas at school.

If you have just been on holiday you might like to make a harbour with matchbox boats and a lighthouse.

How about having some aeroplanes gliding about? Aircraft mobiles are quite easy to make, as you can see from one of the drawings.

Get ideas from your storybooks too. Try a Red Indian camp with wigwams and canoes, or a ranch-house with one or two stockyards beside it.

AIRCRAFT MOBILE

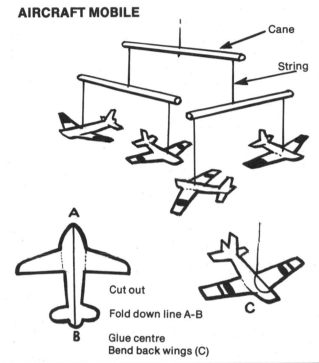

Cane

String

A

Cut out

Fold down line A-B

B

Glue centre
Bend back wings (C)

C

WIGWAM

Draw round saucer
Bend into cone shape
Fix with glue

Cut door

Paint with bright colours

RED INDIAN AND CANOE IN PLASTICINE

Make paddle with stick and card

Matchsticks for head-dress

TREE

Stiff card painted green

Flower puzzle

by Susan Leng

Starting at the letter *D* on the outside of the circle, miss every other letter to find nine garden flowers. When you reach the inner circle, start at the letter *P* and miss every other letter to find eight wild flowers.

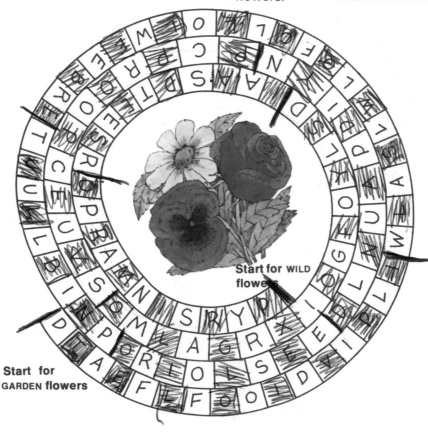

Start for WILD flowers

Start for GARDEN flowers

Model Village

Brownies, Pack Leaders and the Assistant Guider of the 2nd Shottery (St. Andrew's) Pack visit the model village at the beautiful Cotswold township of Bourton-on-the-Water. The village is an exact "Tom Thumb"-size copy of Bourton-on-the-Water, with every house, inn and street perfectly reproduced

Colour slide by Mrs C. M. Richardson

Carnival

The 1st Eastnor Brownies become bearded dwarfs representing "Snow White and the Seven Dwarfs" in a Malvern Carnival tableau

Colour slide by Miss J. Bursnell

Do You Believe in Fairies?

L. Baker Tells You About Some You May Never Have Heard Of

You know about the fairy folk after which Brownie Sixes are named—Pixies, Gnomes, Kelpies, Imps, Elves, Sprites, Leprechauns, and even the Welsh Bwbachod and the Scottish Ghillie Dhu—but do you know of the Ceffyl-Dwr, a Welsh water-horse who has no wings but is able to fly? If you are thinking of looking for one when you visit Wales on holiday it is best to look near pools, where it can sometimes be seen. But beware! Should you manage to mount one you will find it is full of mischief and fun and has a nasty habit of tossing its rider on to the ground. Perhaps it prefers to be ridden by Welsh Brownies!

Many countries have their own magical creatures. The Fuwch Frech, or magic cow, is supposed to be black and brown in colour. She is a fairy cow. Should she hear of someone in great need she will suddenly appear and fill the largest pail in sight with milk. Then she disappears.

The Glaistig is Scottish. It is supposed to be half woman and half goat. If you leave milk out for her she may do your housework for you. She especially likes the company of children and elderly people, so perhaps you could persuade Granny or Grandpa to look out for her with you if you visit Scotland.

is half man and half horse.

A more friendly Scottish creature of legend is the Urisk, who is supposed to be half a man and half a goat. It is supposed to be lucky to see one, and he will often help with farmwork. He is supposed to follow travellers, but has never been known to harm anyone. Urisks are said to meet together in large gatherings in the Highlands from time to time.

The Cesith is a Scottish fairy

As you know, there is supposed to be a monster in Scotland's Loch Ness, but you may not know that Scotland also possesses a Nuckalavee, a horrible sea-monster with poisonous breath. Rather curiously, the Nuckalavee is afraid of running water. If you should happen to catch sight of him you will know him because he

dog with dark-green fur. As his fur blends with the grass in which it hides, the Cesith is hard to find.

Have you ever heard of the Bogie Beast, who can change shape at will and is said to have the power to shrink to nothing or grow as tall as the tree-tops? If you live in Yorkshire you will hear him referred to as the Barguest. He has eyes like burning coals and wears a clanking chain.

Goblin dogs are supposed to be big, black and shaggy and to roam about the countryside at night. As long as you don't touch them they will do you no harm, despite their fierce appearance.

The Pooka is Irish. It is quite harmless, but like all of his kind is full of pranks. He appears mostly as a donkey or horse, but he can change into any shape.

The Hedley Kow is another fairy creature who is fond of changing shape. In spite of its name, it is seldom seen as a cow. A favourite trick it plays is to take the form of a bag of gold. If you happen to stumble on a bag of gold, you will find as you carry it home that it grows heavier and heavier. Put it down and leave it! It's sure to be the Hedley Kow in disguise!

One of the best known legendary creatures is the Dragon, who appears in many fairy-tales. Different countries have different types of Dragon. Some are fierce, some are friendly, some have wings, and some can actually fly without wings. In Eastern countries Dragons always breathe out mist instead of fire, as in Great Britain. Unlike the Dragons of Eastern countries, who are friendly towards people, our Dragons don't like us very much—unless, of course, they can eat us for tea!

This coloured donkey is called Tinkerbell

Donkey

Photographs by Alan T. Band Associates

Pets

Donkeys make delight-
ful pets, but you need
to know how to look
after them and have a
good stable and pad-
dock for them

A rare white donkey with
its mother and their owner

(1) Four Brownies of the 6th Petts Wood West Pack, Kent, paint scenery as part of a Pack Venture for the District pantomime
Photo by Mrs J. Warhurst

Pack
Ventures

(2) The 8th Sutton Coldfield (Maney) Pack's unusual Venture is trying to gain water safety awards. The Brownies work under the helpful eyes of teachers from the Royal Life Saving Society
Photo by Mrs C. R. Randall

Stella and Pat were spending a few days with their farmer uncle before the school autumn term started. Wheat was being cut in Sixteen Acres Field. Men built the sheaves of corn into stooks, which looked like little straw houses. Stella and Pat watched and occasionally lent a hand in fine Brownie fashion.

The two girls, both Brownies, were working for the Pony Rider badge and had taken the opportunity for practice with the old farm ponies.

Today they had taken a tea-basket and some flasks of tea along to Sixteen Acres Field so that work need not stop. It had been a hot day, but they noticed that their uncle kept looking up at the sky.

As they packed the empty flasks and cups into the basket, he came up to them.

"Look, girls," he said, "I want some coupling-pins fetched from the garage at Woodnewton. They were promised for today, but I can't make out what the weather is going to do and I don't want to leave this job till the whole field's cut and stooked. Do you think you could go over and fetch them for me? You could ride Tommy and Fanny. It'll do them good to get some exercise."

Tommy and Fanny were more or less pensioners. Tommy had once pulled the little pony trap, and it was on Fanny that the girls had had their first rides. Now, with more and more use being made of

"Will you ride Tommy and Fanny over to Woodnewton?" asked their uncle

cars and motor-trucks, there was little work for the ponies to do.

Stella and Pat said they would go. They had already ridden the ponies about the farm, but had not been as far as Woodnewton. They felt it would be something of an adventure and rather fancied themselves riding up to the garage on their two ponies and asking for the coupling-pins, as though that sort of thing was an everyday occurrence.

They put the saddles and bridles on the ponies, and Mrs. Reynolds

The Pathfinders

by H. P. Bonser

came over to the stable to make
sure the girths were properly fas-
tened. Stella rode Tommy and Pat
the slightly fatter Fanny.

The way led straight across
Long Meadow and through the
gate into Stonepits Field, then
along by the side of an iron fence
to the bridge over Stony Brook,
thence along a grassy lane and into
the village.

Although the girls persuaded
the ponies into an occasional trot,
their journey was not a very quick
one, and the sun had set before
they started back with the coupling-pins strung over Pat's shoul-
der.

Tommy and Fanny set off down
the lane at a brisker pace now that
their noses were turned homeward.
They crossed the brook and trotted
steadily by the side of the iron
fence towards Long Meadow.
When they came to the gate leading into the meadow Stella and
Pat found to their surprise that all
they could see was a white mist,
which covered the whole of the
meadow.

The farm-buildings with their
windbreak of walnut-trees that
ordinarily made a fine picture on
the horizon were quite blanketed
out. Even the stump of the tree
in the middle of Long Meadow
that had once been struck by
lightning and made a halfway-
across sign was quite lost in the
mist.

This was something the girls
had not bargained for.

"I think I'd better lead Tommy
and see whether I can find the
way," Stella said. "You stick close
to me, Pat."

Stella set off walking in the
direction she thought she ought to
go, the reins over one arm and
Tommy obediently behind.

She walked for a long time, and
both she and Pat began to feel
anxious.

At last Pat shouted, "Look,
Stella, I can see the gate!"

"Thank goodness!" Stella answered. "I thought we were never
going to reach it."

The meadow was cover-
ed in a white mist

Then she stopped in dismay. It wasn't the gate they were looking for at all! It was the one leading from Stonepits Field into Long Meadow that they had come through half an hour before! Stella had simply led them round in a circle and they had come back to the place they started from.

Weary now, Stella climbed up on Tommy's back. She must think things over. Perhaps if they followed the hedge to the corner, and then kept along by the side of Stony Brook . . . but they didn't want to go into the brook!

Tommy lifted his head and sniffed. Fanny did the same. They stood with their necks stretched out for a few moments while the

"Stick close to me, Pat," said Stella, and set off on foot

two girls sat a little bewildered in their saddles; then the ponies set off of their own accord. They walked purposefully and without any sign of hesitation.

"I believe they know the way, Stella," Pat whispered.

"I don't see how they can, Pat. Look at it—just mist, mist, mist! There's not a sound, either, not even a sheep's bleat or the flutter of a bird. We seem to be in a different world from the one we were in this afternoon."

They rode knee to knee, too subdued to talk much. Tommy and Fanny had taken control so quietly that it only dawned slowly on Stella how completely she and Pat had surrendered their authority to the animals.

When she did realise it, it was too late to do anything, for by then they had no idea whereabouts in the field they were—and it was a very big field.

The two ponies kept quietly on, their riders sitting rather soberly and with the reins loose in their hands. It was a sobering thought that with all their human intelligence they were beaten by such a quiet and softly moving element as mist; that they were trusting to the wisdom or instinct of creatures that less than an hour ago they themselves were ordering and guiding.

At length the ponies stopped. The girls could see the gate, and mistily beside the gate the damp branches of a willow-tree.

"It's . . . it's the gate at the home end of Long Meadow," Pat cried, almost unbelievingly.

Stella leant over and unhooked the gate. "You know, Pat," she said, "we've learned something that isn't in the Pony Rider badge test."

"You mean how to find your way through a mist?" Pat nodded. "Yes — leave it to your pony!"

In a few minutes they were climbing the sharp hill towards the farm. The mist thinned as they climbed and they could see the tops of the walnut-trees and the headlights of a car.

The girls shouted and the driver hooted.

"Just coming to look for you. Thought you were lost," called out their uncle.

"Oh, no!" Stella replied.

"No?"

It sounded like a question, but the girls ignored it.

"Here are your coupling-pins, Uncle," said Pat.

But Uncle smiled knowingly to himself when he noticed Stella and Pat slip an extra measure of oats into each of the pony's mangers.

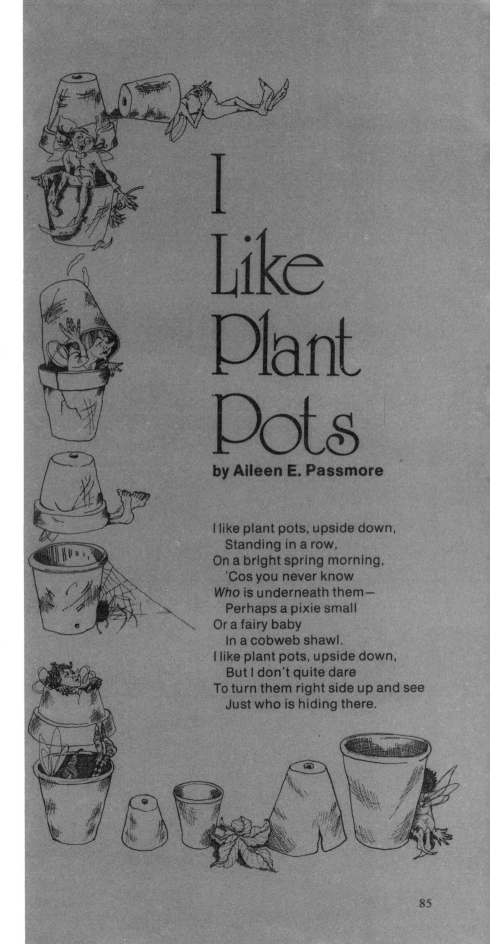

I Like Plant Pots

by Aileen E. Passmore

I like plant pots, upside down,
  Standing in a row,
On a bright spring morning,
  'Cos you never know
Who is underneath them—
  Perhaps a pixie small
Or a fairy baby
  In a cobweb shawl.
I like plant pots, upside down,
  But I don't quite dare
To turn them right side up and see
  Just who is hiding there.

make a matchbox horse

L. J. Hubbard Shows You How

All you need to make this horsy model are a cigarette packet, a matchbox, silver paper, sticky tape, and short lengths of wool.

The drawings on this page will show you clearly how to complete the model.

SNIP TAIL

GOLD OR SILVER PAPER SADDLE FIXED WITH TAPE

SELLOTAPE

TRAY

MATCHES

FEED STRIPS INTO TOP AND BOTTOM EDGES OF MATCH BOX, MAKE CREASES AS INDICATED.

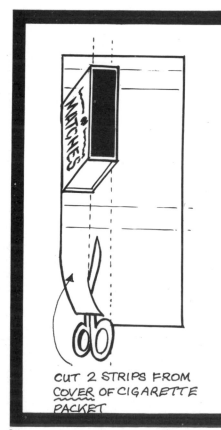

CUT 2 STRIPS FROM COVER OF CIGARETTE PACKET

WOOL

THE FINISHED MODEL

The 1st and 2nd Mable-thorpe Packs dress up in the national costumes of countries of the East and West—China and Germany. The costumes were made by the Brownie Guider, Mrs H. Boughen, and the Assistant Brownie Guider, Mrs M. Burgess

Brownies of the

East and West

Photographs by Mrs. H. Boughen

Miss Muffet: I'm giving a party,
            And soon, I feel sure,
            My guests will be knocking
            Rat-rat! on the door
She skips round the room clapping her hands

Miss Muffet: The tea is all ready—
            The table is laid
            With biscuits and jellies
            And sweet lemonade!

Enter Spider, running towards Miss Muffet
Spider: May *I* be a guest at
            Your party today?
            Please, Little Miss Muffet,
            Do tell me I may!

Miss Muffet *(in alarm)*:
            Oh, dear, a big spider!
            He frightens me so!
            I'll hide in the cupboard,
            Then maybe he'll go.
Exit Miss Muffet, running.
There is a loud knock on the door.
Enter Nursery Rhyme Folk

Miss Muffet'

A Playlet in Rhyme

Nursery Rhyme Folk (all together):
            Hello, dear Miss Muffet!
            We've come, as you see!

They look round in surprise
            But where is Miss Muffet
            Now, where can she be?
Boy Blue: The tea is all ready,
            The fire's burning bright
Jack and Jill: But Little Miss Muffet
            Is nowhere in sight!

Party

ileen B. Edge

Spider: Please, everyone, listen!
         I've something to say—
         I fear that *I* frightened
         Miss Muffet away!

Bo-Peep (shaking her head):
         Oh, dear, you were naughty
         To frighten her so!

Boy Blue: But where, Mr. Spider,
         Did Miss Muffet go?

Spider (pointing off-stage):
         Towards the big cupboard
         She ran off to hide.
         Just open the door and
         You'll see her inside!

*Exit Boy Blue. Re-enter Boy Blue,
leading Miss Muffet by the hand*

Miss Muffet: My guests have arrived, and
         My party's begun.
               . . . .

Spider (coaxingly):
         Please let me stay also
         And join in the fun!

Miss Muffet: Then stay, Mr. Spider.
         'Twas silly of me
         To hide in the cupboard.
         Now let's all have tea!

All join hands and dance round in a ring

All together: Now everyone's happy,
         We're merry and gay!
         Three cheers for Miss Muffet—
         Hip, hip, hip, hurray!

CURTAIN

Calling All Signallers

by Alma Taye

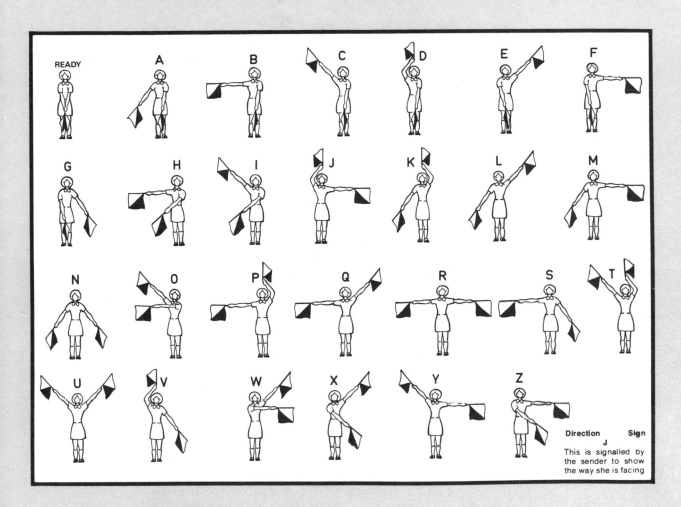

Direction Sign
J
This is signalled by
the sender to show
the way she is facing

The Semaphore Alphabet

Have you ever thought how many times a day we make signals and how many times a day a sign or a sound takes the place of words?

That shake Mother gives you in the morning when you are cosily curled up in bed tells you it's time to get up! That wave you give to your friend over the road says "Hello!" to her, and that knock you give on someone's door is a signal to someone inside to open it.

People have talked to each other with signs from the earliest times. One of the earliest ways of sending a message over a distance quickly was by beacon and smoke. You have all seen in cowboy films tribes of Red Indians sending up smoke-cloud signals that could be seen miles away.

When men went to sea in sailing-ships they had to have some way of sending messages across the water. First of all, sails and flag signals were used, and lights at night. Semaphore, as Brownies know, was used a lot at sea, but as men travelled farther and wider over the oceans of the world they found it was not much use wagging flags at someone who did not speak the same language! So semaphore was adapted for use by any sailor, no matter what country he came from or what language he spoke. So now the International Signal Code is used, and every ship that sails the seven seas has a Code book giving the meanings of every arrangement of flags in the Code.

When Nelson had his famous message signalled from his ship the *Victory* before the Battle of Trafalgar the signallers had to work fast and hard. To say "England expects that every man will do his duty" took thirty-one flags by the signalling code that was used in the year 1805!

The Morse Code

Samuel F. B. Morse, an American, wanted to send messages for miles, much farther than hand-signals could reach. He began to wonder how he could send messages by electricity. Then he had the idea of making dots and dashes mean letters and words. So he invented the code known after him as the Morse Code. It was through his efforts that the first telegraph line in America was set up. This was between Washington and Baltimore. If Samuel Morse could have looked into the future he would have seen that years later, on December 12th, 1901, another famous inventor, Marconi, would receive the letter S of the Morse Code right across 2,000 miles of the Atlantic Ocean. This proved that messages could also be "bent" and sent *round* the earth. With your semaphore flags, even if you could see so far, you would not be able to get high enough to see over the horizon, would you?

Gradually everything has speeded up—on land and sea and in the air. So means of signalling have had to keep pace.

One of the new ways of "signalling" is the teleprinter. It is something like a typewriter and taps out messages that another machine miles and miles away actually prints word for word.

Radio and telephone are valuable means of carrying messages over long distances. The 999 signal over the telephone will alert the police or the fire brigade or the ambulance service, and another telephone signal will tell us the time or what the weather is going to be. Radio messages can control police-cars, ships and aircraft.

Signals Mean Safety

In the ordinary life of us all, signals are important too. Whether we get to our proper destination when we go on a train, boat or aircraft depends much on the correct signals being given— and read—by all concerned. As you know, the signalling system of the railways is by "arms" and, at night, by lights. Traffic signals on roads in red, amber and green lights tell the motorist to stop or go.

Signals From Space

At Jodrell Bank, in Cheshire, stands a giant telescope. A radio wave from this can carry a message to the moon and be received back on earth again. Someone says "Hullo," and that word travels nearly half a million miles. It "bounces" off the moon's surface and is heard on earth two and a half seconds later. Now scientists put satellites into space, and can "bounce" messages from them to all parts of the earth.

But remember, Brownies, you may not be able to use these wonderful ways of sending a message when you most want to, so . . . practise your signalling!

A	· —
B	— · · ·
C	— · — ·
D	— · ·
E	·
F	· · — ·
G	— — ·
H	· · · ·
I	· ·
J	· — — —
K	— · —
L	· — · ·
M	— —
N	— ·
O	— — —
P	· — — ·
Q	— — · —
R	· — ·
S	· · ·
T	—
U	· · —
V	· · · —
W	· — —
X	— · · —
Y	— · — —
Z	— — · ·

The Morse Code

answers to puzzles

P.11
WHICH SIX REACH THE TOADSTOOL?
Sprites.

P.28
THE ISLAND OF FLOWERS
Naval sloop reaches Island of Flowers; pirate ship reaches Green Island, sailing-boat Desert Island, fishing boat Seal Island, galleon Dolphin Island.

P.34
SPIDER'S WEB
Dragon fly, bumble bee, silk worm, daddy longlegs, moth ball, spinning wheel, ants nest, Miss Muffet, Jack Frost, Robert Bruce, silver fish, dust trap. Butterfly is left.

P.34
HIDDEN MESSAGE
1—Needle, 2—trefoil, 3—ironing, 4—toadstool, 5—compass, 6—Thrift, 7—message, 8—Venture, 9—Gardener. *Down:* Lend a Hand.

P.34
MESSAGE IN CODE
Messages are fun this way.

P.35
INTEREST BADGE MAZE
Signaller, Writer, Jester, Craft, Pony Rider.

P.40
WHICH INTEREST BADGE?
Needleworker

P.66
FIND THE ANIMALS
Badger, fox, mole, hedgehog, bat, marten, deer, rabbit, dormouse, weasel, mink, shrew, otter, polecat, hare, vole, stoat, squirrel.

P.76
FLOWER PUZZLE
Garden Flowers: daffodil, wallflower, tulip, rose, lupin, crocus, marigold, aster, pansy. *Wild Flowers:* primrose, daisy, foxglove, poppy, dandelion, bluebell, cowslip, violet.

picture crossword puzzle

To solve this crossword puzzle, look at each picture, then fill in the square across or down that corresponds with the number of that picture.

The grid (as filled in):

2A		4A		6A		1D
	C	²T	O	A	S	³T
⁴R	U	L	E	R		A
	B			A	⁵P	R
⁶E	L	E	P	H	A	N	T
⁸S		I			B	S
⁹P	E	L	I	C	A	N
O		I		A		A
O		E		¹²P	L	A	I	T
¹³N	O	S	E	S		

9A, 12A, 7D, 8D, 5D, 13A, 10D, 11D, 2D, 3D

(Answer key, inverted:)
TOAS
RULER
B D
ELEPHAN
S I
PELICANS
A O
L PLAIE
NOSES

93